Full Contact Leadership

Full Contact Leadership

Dynamic New Ideas and Techniques for Today's Leaders

Wally Schmader

iUniverse, Inc.
New York Lincoln Shanghai

Full Contact Leadership
Dynamic New Ideas and Techniques for Today's Leaders

iUniverse books may be ordered through booksellers or by contacting:

iUniverse
2021 Pine Lake Road, Suite 100
Lincoln, NE 68512
www.iuniverse.com
1-800-Authors (1-800-288-4677)

ISBN-13: 978-0-595-40592-3 (pbk)
ISBN-13: 978-0-595-84958-1 (ebk)
ISBN-10: 0-595-40592-4 (pbk)
ISBN-10: 0-595-84958-X (ebk)

Printed in the United States of America

This book is dedicated to Ronda, Sarah and Jake. Jake and Sarah for giving me daily inspiration and helping me to re-live some of life's lessons through their eyes. Ronda for all of the joy, beauty and texture she has brought to my "Mulligan" life.

I would also like to thank all of the professional leaders I have had the opportunity to work with and learn from through the years. I truly appreciate all of the camaraderie, all of the challenges and all of the fun we have experienced together.

Contents

Introduction

How do managers successfully lead their teams in this complex modern business world? A world where more people can quote Gordon Gecko and Kenneth Lay than Dale Carnegie and Peter Drucker. A world where benchmarking and outsourcing have narrowed the differences between companies to the point where the word "commodity" is used in ways the business leaders of the past would have never imagined. A world where layoffs, furloughs and downsizings have displaced more skilled "white collar" workers than any other time in history and where market volatility has created a new generation of "yes-men" and women who don't feel like they can safely stick their necks out. All this is true and yet, in spite of this environment or perhaps because of it, there may actually be more opportunity for real leaders then ever.

History repeats itself. This is as true in business as it is in any other realm. Business history has shown that the only sustainable advantage that one company can have over another is a "people advantage". Even firms that create real technology or innovation advantages can only rise to the talent and inspiration level of their people. Talented people make all this difference in business and always have. Talented people have all of the ideas, cause all of the change, invest all of the energy, create all of the enthusiasm and are responsible for all of the momentum that a company does (or does not) have. A corollary to that truth is that untalented, uninspired and uncreative management can ruin any company, department or branch. There is case study after case study that show that even in the best circumstances (a great product or service, lack of competition, etc.) poorly managed companies can and will fail or under perform to a degree that would have to be considered as failure.

People make the difference in organizations. People with talent make the difference and developing the ability to identify, develop, manage, retain and inspire talented people has always been the greatest challenge in the business world. This is why leadership is the critical key to building and sustaining successful organizations.

Leadership is the multiplier. Leadership is the difference-maker. Leadership is the point of leverage that can make a business great. Leadership is like the first number in the combination lock. All the others can be right but it does not make any difference if the leadership is wrong.

Thankfully, leadership is a subject that has had a lot of attention. It is not lost on anyone in the business world that the leader is the X-factor. There has been a great debate over whether leadership can be taught. Because of its close association with traits like charisma and vision, leadership is often seen as a purely esoteric subject. It is seen as more of a personality trait and less of a skill. Leadership is often discussed as something you "are" instead of something you do.

I take exception to this sort of leadership discourse. I believe that leadership can be very practical, as practical as any trade. There are esoteric aspects to being a doctor, a welder, a teacher or an architect. But in the end the doctor, the welder, the teacher and the architect must answer to their results. They must be able to "do" something well to succeed in their fields. This is the same with leadership. Even a leader blessed with all of the charisma or vision in the world must eventually get down to business and make something happen. If they don't, they are nothing more than a leadership caricature. A figurehead.

The notion of leadership has been successfully studied and defined by many very credible people over the years. I am partial to the definitions put forth by Warren Bennis, Tom Peters and (of course) Peter Drucker. I don't think leadership needs any more defining. Great work has already been done on that subject and that work is already on the required-reading list of anyone serious about leading people. I do believe, however, that the study of leadership needs to be de-mystified and to be made more practical. We need to quit spending so much energy figuring out the differences between leadership and management and spend more time discovering how real leaders can manage success-fully. Can you lead from behind a desk? Can you lead people who are doing a job you have never done? Can you lead with data? Can you lead the people who are managing you? Can you lead people who don't trust you? Can you lead people you don't know? These are questions worth answering.

The objective of this book is to help you transcend the esoteric aspects of leadership and get to the practical essence of it. We won't be discuss-ing your "leadership image" or your "management style". Rather, the chapters of this book will center on the practicals of leadership. We will focus on how we can use our whole selves to get results through people. Using our "whole self" means considering all of the ways we can con-nect with and understand people. All of the ways we can influence and direct people without manipulation. Collectively, I will refer to these ideas and techniques as Full Contact Leadership. I believe that Full Contact Leadership is the best way to get important things done through people. The goal of this book is to give you both a philosophi-cal and practical understanding of what a Full Contact Leader is, and how you can become one.

Origins

This book has taken shape over several years. It is an accumulation of notes written on scraps of paper, envelopes, margins of ledger pads, napkins and dozens of notebooks I have used to collect high-impact ideas and techniques throughout my life as a leader. These chapters first took form as my attempt to get all of my most important notes in one place. It was only after I had received some positive feedback that I decided to "go public" with my private learnings and thoughts on leadership.

One of the most important goals I have for this book is that it will add to your "leadership vocabulary". A leader should have a constantly growing inventory of descriptions and phrases that they can use to influence the people they are responsible to. Nothing is worse than the leader or manager who is still saying things in the exact same way they did "back in the day". This kind of limitation makes it immediately clear to everyone that they are not learning anything new and may have actually peaked as a leader long ago. How embarrassing would that be if you were that leader? How unfortunate would it be if you were the follower?

A leader with a growing mastery of high-impact words and descriptions will be able to affect more people. One of the central responsibilities of leadership is the responsibility to get better over time. To learn how to better understand why and how people improve and how you can accelerate that improvement. To learn how to work effectively with different kinds of people and in different circumstances. I hope to be able to add several very practical techniques and descriptions to your inventory though this book. It is my hope that you can readily put them into practice and experience the same positive outcomes that I have.

Early Lessons

As a child I moved around a lot. My father worked for Western Electric and was involved in new installations of large-scale telephone equipment. We moved all over while he was doing this kind of work. I learned a lot from these moves. I learned about breaking into new groups. I learned how a person can actually decide what group they were going to belong to after moving into a new situation. I learned that simply being "new" to the others gives you a certain novelty and influence, at least for a while. All of these lessons have proven to be instructive in my life in business.

It was during one of these moves that I got my first memorable lesson in motivation. I was living in New Mexico as a third grader and learned we would be moving to St. Charles Illinois, a Chicago suburb. I had occasionally gotten into classroom trouble in New Mexico with my teacher, usually by talking too much (which is still my most frequent way of getting into trouble today). My teacher would punish offending students by making them clean chalk erasers by pounding them on the outside of our brick school building. She would say, "Gather up the erasers" and you would knew exactly what she meant. I would hang my head, go outside with the erasers, and start pounding.

Once we arrived in Chicago I started school immediately, still in the third grade. In just a day or two I observed something very interesting. When kids in my class behaved very well (finished a test in a timely way, were helpful to another classmates, etc.) we were *allowed* to go outside and clean the erasers. The teacher would say; "Carl, I really appreciate how you helped Sandra. Why don't you take the erasers outside and clean them?" Carl would get a big smile on his face and be out the door and into the cold winter air to clean the erasers as a reward for good behavior. I was struck even then about how this act was seen as either good or bad based solely on the teacher's delivery of it.

It was a useful lesson for me. I went on to realize many other early lessons on management, motivation and manipulation. Like many of you, most of my early experiences with management came in the retail world. The hourly-wage world of retail is where many people first learn to distrust their leaders and managers. For many people, their first fast-food or mall job is the first time they have ever been managed by someone who does not necessarily have their best interest at heart. Previous to those first jobs we are being managed and led by teachers, siblings, camp counselors and parents. Many people carry those early negative images of "management" through their whole working lives.

It has always been interesting to me that most people's first positive job experiences come with their first merit-based position. Yet these kinds of jobs are not usually available to young people. It would be great if we could get young people "off the clock" so that they could feel the pride that comes with being paid more for doing a good job and the consequence of being paid less (or not at all) for doing bad work. It is how the real world works but, regrettably, most of us get used to being paid for time. This lays the groundwork for some bad habits and a native distrust of managers. It is because of these early experiences most of us end up with one or both of the following stuck in our heads:

Management = Manipulation

Management = Getting people to do things they don't want to do

Of course, the successful management of people requires much more of us as leaders than simple manipulation or direct motivation. It requires us to "be" something for our teams. It requires that we know them and understand why they are in our organizations at all. It requires us to be a leader.

Many capable leaders seem to disengage emotionally as they move up the corporate ladder and take on more responsibilities. In some organizations this disengagement is almost like a rite of passage. As you move from being one of "them" (the worker bees) to one of "us" (the Leadership team, with a capital "L") you detach yourself from the drama and volatility that is part of every day business. You learn to keep it at arm's length. That's not for you anymore; you're an executive. There are businesses I have been involved with where the "suits" actually take on kind of bemused manner when they talk about the people that are doing the work that keep the business rolling along. It is a form of condescension that is palpable to everyone. Needless to say, this kind of egotism is certainly not Full Contact Leadership.

Think about the leaders that you have known who have managed to bring their hearts and souls into the executive's office with them. They maintained the ability to feel the emotions that are a part any high-performing team. This is a rare leader who can stay connected in this way even as they have to consider and be responsive to larger-scale issues across their business. This is a form of humility that is very hard to find in leaders. It is very valuable and powerful. The ability to emotionally connect with people at all different levels of the organization is a personality hallmark of the Full Contact Leader and will be discussed in other chapters of the book.

Objectives

Throughout the chapters of this book I will attempt to help you build yourself into a better and more effective leader. I will share with you several important philosophies and techniques that you will be able to use in very practical ways.

I hope to help you deepen your skill-set and broaden your understanding of how and why people perform successfully in team environments. We will discuss how "working on yourself" can be a powerful way to leverage performance in your organization and why all meaningful improvement starts with you, the leader.

I will try to help you see some of the roadblocks that can negatively influence your success as a leader. We will discuss rationalization, manipulation, over-dependence on numbers, false superiority, cynicism…some of the many layers that can build up between leaders and their teams. It is this process of opening yourself up to self-improvement and new ideas that is at the essence of being a Full Contact Leader.

What is a Full Contact Leader? A Full Contact Leader is the leader of the future. He is the leader who can answer to the challenge of remaining authentic to them selves while successfully leading others. Full Contact Leadership is about stripping away all that comes between leaders and the people they are responsible to. Removing all of the biases, all of the manipulation, all of the "boss" imagery and all of the stereotypes to get to the practical matter of leading people successfully.

Full Contact Leaders learn new ways of relating to their followers. They are constantly upgrading their "leadership vocabulary" to increase the quality and effectiveness of their communication. Because they are more substantial as leaders, they are able to produce exceptional results without resorting to manipulation.

A Full Contact Leader is a leader who assumes the best in people and is anxious to learn new techniques that will help him develop his team. A Full Contact Leader does not look for shortcuts and is prepared to work on him or herself first to drive extraordinary business results. Through the chapters in this book I will endeavor to help you to do exactly that.

Working on Yourself

Most of the prevailing ideas we all have about management and leadership are rooted in one overriding concept. That concept is that good managers and leaders are good because they know how to get people to do the things that they need to do for the company, department, district, etc. to succeed. When we call ourselves "managers" or "leaders" we automatically begin to define ourselves by the impact we have on others. It is certainly true a manager who can effectively organize and direct people's efforts and activities will be seen as a successful manager. Because of these obvious truths the impact of "working on yourself" is sometimes lost or under-emphasized. Most contemporary management discourse is missing this most powerful and reliable way to improve your business. The idea of self-improvement as a growth strategy is not often discussed.

"Working on yourself" means purposely doing and learning things that will make you a better leader, manager or person. Most of the really classic business literature is intensely focused on this idea but, regrettably, the topic of self-improvement has for the most part migrated from the business section of the bookstore and re-rooted itself in the psychology and self-help isle. Most of the books you can find in your bookstore's self-improvement section are dedicated to currently popular syndromes, behavioral explanations and relationship strategies. The best of them are aimed at self-understanding more than self-improvement. The worst of them actually focus on teaching people how to manipulate their self-images or teach readers to hide from the responsibility for personal development with accountability-shifting ideas and concepts.

Why has this shift away from self-improvement as a way to succeed in business happened? There are many reasons. One is that we, as managers, simply prefer to think that big improvements will come from other people changing rather than thinking that we can (and should) change and grow ourselves to actualize business gains. Another reason may be that we forget that *we* are the constants in our careers and businesses. There is going to be considerable and constant change and churn in most modern organizations. The truth is that when you are managing in today's volatile workplace you will usually do best by managing the constants instead of the variables, and that starts with you.

Perhaps a valuable core belief would be that that we could all expect bigger outcomes, bigger opportunities, bigger leverage points and bigger possibilities if we focused on becoming bigger people. This belief says that over time I can actually increase my *capacity* to lead, and in doing so; increase the possibilities of my organization. Capacity is one of the biggest words in business and it is not changed easily. When it is successfully affected, a leader has every right to confidently expect better results. In what areas can our capacity actually be increased? What follows is a short list of personal abilities and capacities that can be influenced by active self-improvement.

- The ability to work with different kinds of people.
- The ability to deal with crisis.
- The capacity to adapt to change.
- The improvement of ones communication skills and vocabulary.
- The capacity to be innovative.

- The capacity to care.

- Physical, intellectual and emotional stamina.

- Listening skills.

- Anticipatory learning (what should I be learning now to succeed next year or five years from now?).

- The ability to work with a new technology.

- The capacity for high expectations.

There are also other many other less obvious benefits to working on your self. Think of it this way: you will probably be as capable or less capable (aging does not always help) in your work five years from now unless you take overt steps in the other direction. Without steps in the direction of purposeful self-improvement you will be the same in five years except for the people you meet, the things you learn, the books you read and the experiences you allow yourself to be influenced by. By deciding in advance how you will be different in five years you take control of how, and in what form, you will be presenting your self in the future. It is a powerful concept.

Another huge benefit of active self-improvement is the opportunity to make it a priority with your team. Setting a personal example and then teaching self-improvement skills to your people gives you a chance to multiply all of the positive effects than can come from your active self-improvement. I cannot imagine a more powerful way to improve a team while building loyalty and appreciation than making it clear (in words and deeds) that your organization is one where self-improvement will be a cornerstone. Most of us have had a boss, coach or teacher along the way who would not accept that we were working at our full potential and insisted and expected us to improve and develop. What an impact such a person can have. Great leaders should see their people as being growing, developing and improving parts of a team. We should expect them to get bigger and more capable the longer we get to work with them. What a compliment to can give another person, to see their capability as being unlimited.

I would contend that a student-leader is also more attractive to followers than a leader who presents her self as a finished product. What is more attractive in a leader than humility? It is notable that there is a kind of "humility curve" in most organizations. Think about the places you have worked and the people you have had around you. Typically newer and less accomplished the leader is, the less humble they are. At the top of most very successful organizations you will find leaders who have learned the importance of humility. You can almost make a case that it is not possible to rise up through an organization and lead successfully for the long term without the ability to demonstrate real humility. Many of the least humble leaders I have met over the years were actually placed into their positions through a political process, nepotism or questionable leverage. Most of the "celebrity CEO's" we have met through the media have obvious humility gaps that nearly-always lead to their eventual fall. It has become a source of entertainment for me to, when I meet a leader who seems to be absent of humility, to find out how they got their position. It is typically not an up-through-the-ranks or "school of hard knocks" track that led them there. Any grandmother could tell us that being humble makes other people pull for us and wish us well. We will discuss the topic of humility in more detail later in this chapter. The bottom line is that being egocentric and having a lack of basic humility causes people to wish and act against us. It is as simple as that.

What are some of the things we as leaders and managers can do to increase our capacities for success? Let's discuss a few of the best.

Acting like the Person You Want to Become

The best piece of self-development advice I ever got was from a top-notch leader whose name is Chuck Reddick. Chuck was incredibly influential in my career, especially when I was a very young man. I had never met anyone who had the presence that Chuck had. Like many gifted speakers he was able to command the attention of everyone when he was in front of a large group. What made Chuck especially unique were his one-on-one communication skills. When Chuck sat in front of you it was like you were the only person in the world. At the time he was also the most successful manager in our companies history. Over time I got very close to Chuck and our careers were intertwined for many of the succeeding years. Chuck's business acumen was daunting for a young person who was new to the world of business. He made it his primary objective to let me and all of his team know that any of us could have all of his success and more. How? We wondered. "Because I *learned* how to lead" Chuck said. He would recommend book after book, tape series after tape series and seminar after seminar. The more ambitious of us took it all in and plowed through any self-improvement material we could get our hands on. I literally read hundreds of books and articles during that period. There was a period of time where when someone quoted or referred to nearly any book or business article I knew what they were going to say before they said it.

The fact that Chuck insisted on referring to himself as a self-made leader (rather than a "born" leader like an ego-centric person might have done) inspired me to try to become that myself. To actually set about learning the things I would need to know to become an effective leader of people. The most simple and effective piece of advice I ever got from Chuck was this: Act now like the person you want to become. It was a twist on the famous Earl Nightingale maxim that you become what you think about. This idea had a huge impact on me because, even though I was frequently confused and unsure of myself in my present form, I always knew what the person I wanted to become would do. I knew what they would say, how they would respond and what they would value. Acting like the person you would like to become insures that you are always in touch with your highest level of capability, and that you are always responding as your best self. Over time you must actually, and permanently, become the person you wanted to be.

Over time I realized that this idea worked in all of my most important roles. As a husband and as a parent, "acting like the (insert role) I wanted to become" has been a reliable way to answer to my best self in every important role of my life.

Changing Your Mind

The term "changing your mind" has been corrupted with repeated misuse. If you were looking at the words for the first time you would understand them to mean that one has changed their mind on purpose and maybe for the better. In recent years the idea of a people changing their minds has come to be seen as some kind of character flaw. There have been leaders who have been maligned for changing their minds. It has even been a topic in important political campaigns.

Why would changing your mind be bad? Sometimes changing our minds is necessary for growth. Many times it is our minds, and the inflexibility of them, that retards our growth as leaders and people. What is worse that a manager who for ten years uses the same language and anecdotes to communicate with their team? Sometimes changing your mind might just mean rearranging your prejudices. In many cases it is our prejudices that become our performance bottlenecks. I don't mean racial prejudices, although they always cause problems as well. I mean prejudices about what works and what doesn't. What to do in certain situations, and what not to. Changing your mind can mean learning a new way to respond to a situation that you have seen 1,000 times.

These are the situations where changing your mind can be the most effective. Business situations that repeat themselves represent the best opportunities to learn a new response. This kind of learning can make a huge impact on a team that has seen you do it the same way over and over. There is a saying that goes like this: if the only tool you know how to use is a hammer, then everything looks like a nail. Sometimes "changing your mind" just means getting some new tools.

Learn to Quit Rationalizing

Most individuals who find their way into positions of leadership are intelligent people. Usually they have been able to learn very effective interpersonal and political techniques as they have risen in the ranks of their organization. You are probably just this sort of person, smart and relatively flexible in your responses to things. There is one area of leadership where intelligence and experience can actually let you down. It happens when you use your intellect to justify or manipulate your or other people's beliefs about a particular result or outcome. That is the long way to describe the process of rationalizing.

Every personality strength has its corresponding weakness, especially in a business setting. If a leader is reliable and consistent they are probably also resistant or reluctant to change. If a person has a dynamic fiery personality they are also most likely volatile and inconsistent. If a leader is described as an innovative "out of the box" thinker you can bet they are also impatient and may have attention-span challenges. If they are great with people they are often bad with numbers. You get the picture.

The downside to being smart is that you are then capable of rationalizing. Rationalizing is the "dark side" of intelligence. You have to be really sharp to do it effectively. Rationalizing successfully means having the ability to spin an outcome or result in a way that causes the listener (or the rationalizer himself) to draw an inaccurate conclusion. Maybe the best way to understand what rationalizing really is is to simply break the word down: rational/lies.

Rationalizing is hard. It can wear you out. If you are good at it you can become addicted. Some leaders begin to create rationalized conclusions to nearly everything negative that happens in their organizations. The real danger in it is that rationalized conclusions shield people from seeing the truth. If a negative situation or result is rationalized it can simply go away. You can miss the opportunity to learn from it. Furthermore, a leader can miss the opportunity to demonstrate how to be fully accountable to their results. Perhaps the greatest risk is the credibility gap that will surely form around the person who becomes known as a rationalizer. A leader can afford to sometimes be wrong. A leader can be excused from saying the wrong thing occasionally. An authentic leader cannot risk their credibility. Your ethical stance must be non-negotiable. At the bottom line rationalizing is not completely honest, even if you are the only one who knows you are doing it.

The Tyranny of First-Person Pronouns

One of the major changes in how people relate to each other has gone largely undocumented. Like most large-scale trends it has moved slowly and gradually from popular culture into the office. The phenomenon is the incredible over-use of self-referential statements and comments. It is hard to tell how it all started. Perhaps it was Sigmund Freud who got us all thinking about the layers of our personality. He taught us that we actually had different "selves" that operate distinctly from one another.

Maybe it has been the nearly complete media saturation has take place from the 1950's through the present. The personalities we are all trained to love and hate have engaged us all with their sense of self. Politicians, entertainer, athletes…celebrities have been force—fed to us and we cannot be satisfied. There are even "business celebrities" now.

Today it is not unusual at all to hear or participate in a "conversation" where parties only talk about themselves. They don't react to the others thoughts or words but instead simply take turns talking about themselves. It happens all of the time and it is very different from what conversations used to be. I am not a sociologist and I don't understand what all of the roots of this broad change might be. I am not even sure if it is necessarily good or bad.

I do know that it presents an opportunity for a leader to be a completely different type of person. Listen around your office. I guarantee you that the most used words from the bottom to the top of your organizational chart are these: I, me & my. Your administrative assistant is talking about I, me & my. The UPS man is talking about I, me and my. The sales people are talking about I, me and my. It has gotten so bad that now you can be considered a polite conversationalist if you can just avoid interrupting the other person with your next statement or opinion. The "pregnant pause" before speaking that many successful leaders used to emphasize their words has all but disappeared. Listen to some conversations around you. What you will hear are people, so anxious to talk, that they habitually talk over what they think will be the last few words of the sentence spoken by the person they are in "conversation" with.

The leadership opportunity in this is obvious. You can be the person who successful changes their communication channel. You could be the leader or manager who successfully gets out of the "me" business and begins to invest his communication opportunities in "let's", "we", and "our." The payoff? You will engage easier and you will then have unlimited opportunities to show interest and concern for the people you are communicating with. You will quickly see an upward shift in how you perceive conversations. (1) What was noise can become substantive. (2) When you decide to state a belief, a question, an observation or an opinion you will be heard.

You will quickly feel a transition take place from the "taking turns talking" conversation model (where the conversation generally needs to be repeated more than once for even the smallest result to surface), to actual conversations. Gradually you will begin to realize the people you are talking with are not just watching your mouth move while they think of what they are going to say next, they are actually listening. By persistently using "we", "let's", "our" and "your" in your speech you are engaging people in a conversational collective. It is not necessary for them to quickly spit out their next "I", "me" or "my" statement. The more senior you are to the person you are speaking with, the more meaning and impact this kind of conversation has.

Here are a few recommendations to help you break away from the first-person-pronoun conversation style:

- Consciously try not to say the words "I", "me" and "my". They are necessary words, and you will use them, but some awareness of frequency will help.

- Let a moment pass after someone has made a comment. This is the "pregnant pause". In this way they know that you are not simply waiting for your turn to talk. A pause will also add some weight to whatever you are going to say.

- Use lots of clarifying phrases and questions like: "I understand", "why do you feel that way?", "OK", "Is there anything else you want to say?" Imagine you are going to be quizzed on what the other person is saying once they are done speaking.

- Practice with your family and in social situations. Good conversationalists are very rare people today. No one would appreciate it more than your spouse or kids. It has been said that the best way to be interesting is to be interested. No one has ever made a bad impression by listening.

The Power of Humility

One of the other interesting results of the self-promoting that is so prevalent today is its nearly complete failure to do what it is suppose to do: make you look good. We have all become so inventive and fixated on self-promotion and self-referential commentary that we all know when it is being done and what the speaker is trying to accomplish. We have grown up with it and it is transparent to everyone. That is what makes the compulsion so ironic; everyone in the room can tell when a speaker is trying to direct attention to him or herself. And it is not attractive. There was a time when the same could be said of overt modesty. There was a whole generation influenced by a few genuinely modest and seemingly-gracious celebrities (think Steve Allen, Dean Martin, Joe DiMaggio, Johnny Carson, Dolly Parton, Jack Nicklaus and Billy Graham).

These were very successful people being very modest and self-deprecating. Just like today everyone wanted to be like the celebrities they loved the most and everyone began to use overt modesty as a way to attract attention to them selves. Over time, it became as obvious as all of the thinly veiled self-promotion is today. Today you will still meet people of that generation who are compulsive in their false modesty.

I am not sure if these personality traits change in broad cycles or if they are driven by celebrities and popular culture. What I do know is that authentic and true humility, especially in a leader, is an incredibility attractive and powerful trait.

What is "authentic humility?" It is simply true humility. Being truly humble about one's self and one's accomplishments. It means sincerely sharing credit and managing overblown praise. Authentic humility is also the ability to accept congratulations and compliments humbly and with gratitude. Refusing sincere compliments is not a sign of humility. Accept what you deserve, be grateful for it and share credit when it is proper and accurate to do so. Humility means that you appear to be neither bigger nor smaller than you actually are. You are exactly what you appear to be, nothing more and nothing less. It is an admirable and powerful character trait and worthy of your study and aspiration.

Be a Tree

Consider a large tree. Think about how it got to be so big. I think a great leader can be likened to a great tree. Botanists tell us that some large trees have root systems that are as large or larger than the part of the tree that is above the ground. They say that is takes an incredibly widespread network of roots to nourish a large tree. Look at a big oak or maple tree and imagine the root system beneath the ground to be as large as the trunk, branches and leaves that appear above it. It is amazing to think about, isn't it? Clearly the "tree" is actually the whole thing. It is what appears above and below the soil. In fact, it is the growth below the soil that will dictate how large any tree can grow above it.

This is exactly the way great leaders are. They are way more substantial beneath the surface than they superficially appear to be above it. Their roots go deep and it is these roots of learning and experience that have allowed them to be who they are. As you come to know a substantial leader you realize just how deep their roots go. Be the kind of leader who works on their roots (knowledge, reputation, understanding & sensitivity) just as much as they work on the leaves (appearance, promotion & ego). The next time you see a great tree, consider how big it must be beneath the surface and strive for the same balance in your self.

Develop an Appetite for Change

It has been said many times that the only constant in this world is change. This is especially true in business, where change is ever accelerating and impossible to ignore. There are very few people who actually seek out change. Most of us would rather face change only when we have to. Even then, it is not welcome. Because change is inevitable, it makes sense for leaders to re-evaluate their relationship with it. When leaders think deeply about change they often realize that most of the most painful or uncomfortable changes they have experienced actually worked out to be positive and, in most cases at least, improved their overall condition.

Being a successful leader requires persistent self-development and active change. It is like looking into a kaleidoscope. You are constantly turning and seeing new things. Occasionally you will come upon a beautiful pattern and want to keep looking at it for a while, but life and leadership requires you to keep turning. Sometimes you will want to try to turn the kaleidoscope back to see a pattern you remember and love, but you can never find the exact pattern by going back. You must keep turning to see all of the colors and possibilities available to you.

Working on your self means being willing to see yourself as a "work in progress". To know that you will be more tomorrow than you are today. It means you should be willing to shed certain habits and predispositions that may have become second nature for you. The payoff for emphasizing self-improvement in your personal and business lives is the ultimate payoff: becoming a more substantial and capable person.

Success Events

The ability to "catch people doing it right" is at the forefront of all leadership attributes. It is central to the desire to positively reinforce actions that we, as managers and leaders, want to see repeated by the people on our teams. Unenlightened or under-skilled leaders tend to focus on the things that their team members *don't* know and the actions they *don't* take, thus reinforcing these failing images in the minds of the people they are paid to help. Any leader who can become good at picking up on and recognizing the many little actions and decisions that lead to long term success will see his team consistently develop as (one by one) he builds positive and reinforcing relationships with the individuals on his team. This kind of focus on people is so critical to successful leadership that we have even developed a sort of compensation vocabulary to describe it. We routinely use terms like *paying* attention, *rewarding* with recognition and *spending* time which actually sound like financial compensation and show the importance of a positive focus on people.

Let's discuss what kinds of things we can pay attention to as we help our people build their self-images as improving and succeeding professionals on a high performance team. It is our job to look for and find what I have come to call "Success Events". These are the many little and big things that happen along the way when someone is becoming successful in their particular job. It does not matter if the person we are trying to build is an executive or an assembly line worker. The principals are the same. These events break down into three general categories.

1. Performance Events (successful outcomes).

2. Effort Events (demonstrations of hard work and persistence).

3. Attitude Events (exhibitions of a positive attitude and commitment to what we are trying to do together).

I want to discuss "Success Events" of each type so together we can get better at seeing these events when they happen and be able to respond to and recognize them properly.

Performance Events

This is the easiest area to pay attention to because this category focuses on results. Those leaders who are good at positive reinforcement and recognition usually focus exclusively in this area. It the easiest to measure and is almost always very visable to management. Every kind of successful result can (and should) be recognized. Results like sales, service victories, documented improvements, customer commendations, hitting or exceeding desired targets, promotions and every other kind of positive result should be paid attention to. Most companies make an effort to recognize performance, they just don't take it far enough. Usually firms only recognize efforts that have a direct affect on revenue or customer satisfaction.

There are specialists and role-players all over your organizations who do a great job every day and would be sorely missed if they were no longer part of the team (even if they are in a low-profile job). Does your office have a receptionist that is never late? You would certainly notice if he was constantly late, how about some recognition for reliability? Does your mailroom run like clockwork? Who's responsible for that excellence? Why is there never trash in the parking lot? Someone is doing a great job. You don't remember the last time your company intranet crashed? It sounds like there is somebody performing there too. Are the paychecks always correct and on time? That is somebody's job, and they are doing it well. Are company reports and newsletters consistently professional and free of errors? Again, someone is performing at a high level. Think about the things that would truly be a problem if they were not done well and seek out the people who keep them running smoothly. Paying attention to solid performance is never a mistake. Look for it on all levels.

Effort Events

This is the "cause" part of the cause-and-effect equation. We want to be diligent in the attention we pay to efforts that we know will lead to meaningful results. The results are usually seen as their own rewards, so being finely tuned into to the efforts our team members are making is a key leadership element. A big sale, a key improvement, a deadline met or an exceptional outcome is always the result of some unique effort made by some body. It is especially important to recognize quality effort when the result is not clear to everyone. Pay attention to effort as a key leading indicator because this is exactly what it is, wherever you find it.

Clear examples of sincere effort are participation in office work, team members working on themselves though seminars or continuing educa-tion, staying late or arriving early, aiding someone outside their depart-ment...there are a million examples that can be seen, appreciated and properly recognized. Anything above and beyond a person's norm can and should be acknowledged. Remember; intelligent effort or "above-and-beyond" contributions should never go unrecognized. Not recog-nizing those kinds of heroics send a message that is just as clear as when you do actually take the time to pay the proper kind of attention to effort.

Attitude and Commitment Events

These are the events and actions that convey a person's belief in themselves and/or their commitment to the team. These actions are not always overt or obvious. A leader must have their antennae finely tuned to catch these kinds of recognition opportunities. They are easy to miss and yet they are so very important. Some good examples of attitude and commitment events are; a team member buying a new business book or outfit, a very enthusiastic interaction with a client, someone seeking out the right influences, quality input from and unlikely source, written and shared personal goals, heavy involvement in a meeting, encouraging a friend or relative to apply for a job in your organization, attending a seminar or meeting that requires an investment of time or money and many, many (many) others. These kinds of events are the hardest to spot so the recognition of attitude events is a truly a high-impact form of paying attention.

Providing a place where people can come to be excellent means that we must all learn or re-learn the art of recognition. Here is a timeless (and unbreakable) rule of management: *what gets rewarded, gets repeated.* If that were the only leadership idea you knew you could still succeed as a team builder, manager or parent. Many aspiring leaders do not succeed because they never grasp this rule. Don't let that be you. Recognition is an important part of how we compensate people for their efforts at work. It is one of the most important reasons good people stay in organizations. Many studies have shown that most people rate positive recognition as more important than money when discussing job satisfaction.

Those of us who forget to pay positive attention to their people or "can't find anything good to say" are, in fact, saying plenty. There are great things going on in your organization. If there is not, then you are simply not paying the right kind of attention. Make recognizing Success Events the number one item on your job description.

Trust

The important leap from one performance level to another, for an individual or team, requires a unique form of emotional exposure. This kind of exposure has been labeled many different ways in business literature. For our purposes let's just say that this leap, once taken, opens up all the possibilities for an improvement-oriented person or team. As a leader in any kind of organization, it is our job to jump frequently and publicly in the way that we would want others to. This leap of commitment can take different forms. A leader who jumps with a net is called "reliable". A leader who jumps without a net is called a maverick or even irresponsible. A leader who won't jump isn't called a leader at all.

This leap of faith is a requirement necessary for anything extraordinary to take place in any team environment. Any family, business or sports team must be willing to make a collective leap of commitment well in advance of any expected results. Men and women who become good at provoking these intellectual and emotional leaps are the architects of the future and provide the seeds of untold opportunity and success.

The springboard for these kinds of leaps is trust, and I will devote the next few paragraphs explaining why I believe this is so. As we discuss the topic of trust you may prefer to think of it as "belief". For our purposes they are interchangeable. I like the word trust because in this chicken-and-egg relationship, trust is the chicken.

The concept of trust (relative to management) can be broken down into four important areas:

1. Trust in our selves (our instincts and our ability to learn).

2. Trust in our people (if you feel you can't trust the folks you have on your team you are saying much more about yourself than you are about them, see number 1).

3. Trust in the process of growth (this is often a blind trust, unfortunately).

4. Agreement.

Trust is one of the most powerful, and least understood, creative forces necessary for organizational excellence. To fully grasp the advantages and consequences of prioritizing trust I'm going to take these four different types of trust and discuss them as individual topics. It makes more sense this way (trust me).

Trust (Belief) in Ourselves

You, the organizer (manager, leader, etc.) are the foundation of all of the success or failure that can and will occur in your area of responsibility. This being true, we must be able to trust our own intuitive ability to make decisions and trust both the long term and short-term outcomes of these decisions. Often the people above us in our organization will judge our effectiveness by the short-term results of our decisions. In contrast to our superiors, our subordinates will make their judgments based on their estimates or understanding of the long-term results and how these results will affect them personally. This presents a prickly scenario, (for the middle manager especially), and is a reality that clearly sits opposed to the true health of your business, district, department, region or division. It appears that the "talk about the Mission but measure the quarter" paradigm for business is going to make it safely into the 21st century. This is a shame because it (this two-faced way of measuring progress) is certainly responsible for turning at least one generation of would-be leaders largely into a bunch of cynics.

Because of the "you can't please everyone" reality of business, a responsible and well-intentioned leader must please him self first. This decision, to answer to one self first is, in itself, an act of trust. Pleasing oneself is not hard to get excited about. The only drawback being that a "scapegoat-less" manager is going to have trouble finding a big enough rock to hide under when, occasionally and inevitably, their foresight is found to be wanting.

What to do? Be a yes-person to the people one or two layers up, or Mr. Popularity in your own shop? The long-term undesirability of both these choices is what usually inspires our heroes, the independent (and perpetually exposed) free thinkers, to find their own way. By long-term observation and experimentation I have noticed that there are basically two methods of decision-making. Let's discuss them briefly and recognize that our real goal is to have the ability to answer concurrently to the short and long-term ramifications of the decisions and subsequent actions/campaigns. Any big thinking geometrically-mobile modern professional knows that consistently poor decision-making can imperil even the most conservative career path. Yet to have any hope of living up to your own standards and goals the dice must occasionally be rolled. We must take our own philosophical high road and realize it goes straight uphill.

Method A: Reactive Learning

This method is also known as "trial by fire" and "learning from our mistakes". You really don't have a choice in this one. It happens accidentally for reasons that Ivan Pavlov explained to us a long time ago (did you hear a bell?). Reactive learning is very useful in a wide range of business applications and it has the obvious advantage that you can "reactively" learn good lessons from other people's screw-ups. We have all had the experience of watching a really bad idea or execution forever alter someone's reputation or career path. Probably the biggest draw-back of learning exclusively in this reactive way is that you will acquire basically the same lessons, skills and competencies as will anyone else working in a similar environment. Because of this, learning in a reactive way rarely leads to breakthrough implementations or ideas. One notable exception: the invention of the oven mitt.

Method B: Proactive Learning

My understanding of the overused and under-defined word "proactive" is that of "an idea-based decision or action". Applying that definition to the idea of organizational learning leads us to think of being proactive as being a person who can act on instinct and then follow through, all the while accumulating lessons on wins and losses. Interestingly, I have concluded that it is probably better in the long run to have private defeats *and* private victories. Those small accumulated wins form the basis of real trials and experiences that will serve you well when they finally make sense in another situation or context.

The experts have always told us that to improve we must fail frequently and that most ideas become "good" or "bad" based on their timing or execution. Ideas sometimes need to mature and take form under differ-ent circumstances to succeed. The proactive learner tries lots of ideas, avoids marrying any of them, all the while carefully accumulating out-comes and observations for future use. Today's successful innovator cannot afford to have their whole identity or reputation tied to one idea or theme. I really can't imagine anything more important to your future than a long list of (possibly) great ideas awaiting their time.

Leaders for the future are simply leaders that have identified more resources for learning and generating ideas. Use anything and anybody you can to help you in this area. If there is an "intellectual elite" in America it must be because some people put a much higher priority on observation and sensitivity. There is an intellectual subculture that is more into being "interested" than being "interesting". Your own experiences and biases simply won't give you enough raw materials for consistent innovations. Only a real (and purposeful) diversity of backgrounds and experiences can provide the kind of fertile soil you need to make constant improvement a reality. Ideas and mini-breakthroughs are happening all around you all the time. Who can you blame if you don't see them?

Trust in Your People

There are a huge percentage of people (my guess is 60%) in management who have basically postponed the accomplishment of anything meaningful until they have "the right people". I am constantly talking with otherwise capable managers who really believe that there is a certain person or combination of people that he will eventually "find" that will put his organization in the record books forever. This is a deadly belief. Not only is it profoundly incorrect but also it is fundamentally lazy. What about *"developing"* a team or a standout person capable of carrying your torch? The only person he hasn't "found" is the one wearing his pants. People are people and that's the best thing about them. They are smart and ambitious and diverse and energetic and talented and would rather succeed than fail...period. If those beliefs resonate with you then I am certain that you have a great team of hardworking and committed people. If the description above sounds naïve or like wishful thinking to you then I would be willing to bet that you have staff problems that you figure will be solved when you find some of the "right people".

Here's how to turn your people into the "Right People". The first thing to understand is that your team is always a reflection of you. This is clearly for better and for worse. It is our real beliefs and expectations about our people that will dictate our relationships with them and (indirectly) their desire to contribute. What are your beliefs about the people in your organization? Do you believe that every one of them has the capability to succeed and contribute? Do you know what their goals are? Do you believe that the opportunity they have with you is a reasonable means to their career goals? Do you believe that your team is strengthened by it's level of diversity? Are you providing a place where people can come to be excellent? These are all tough questions when they are answered honestly. They are all very important and your desire and ability to be honest with yourself regarding your core beliefs in these areas will govern the speed of your progress as a leader. Here are a couple of disconcerting facts that can help us gain some perspective about "our people".

Disconcerting Fact #1: "Your People" have chosen you from among more alternatives than you have chosen them from.

Disconcerting Fact #2: Your team's performance will impact your career much more than your performance will impact theirs

Understanding these uncomfortable truths will help you to get a handle on the idea of "finding" vs. "developing" people to contribute to your organization. Clearly some people are more able to succeed in certain job situations than others. It should be obvious to all of us that talent, intellect, experience, expectations, motivation and preparation will have a great deal to do with a persons likelihood of making a big impact in any organization. That being said, we must also be open to the fact that these factors mostly exist (or don't exist) independent of active management. It would be a mistake to invest too much of our leadership interest in isolating these attributes alone. We would be better off concentrating our interest and skill in areas that will allow us to differentiate our organization or team from all of the others that a talented, experienced, motivated and prepared individual would surely be able to choose from.

Let's concentrate on providing the best situation possible for a person to succeed in. Let's think creatively about what makes a work situation valuable to the individual who is in it. About ten years into my management career, I became aware of a very simple (aren't they all after you know them?) idea that helped me accelerate my team-building confidence and ability. This concept allowed me to almost immediately be more responsive to the people who I fervently wanted to succeed in their positions. Here it is: *I work for my people's goals.* This seems to me to be the very definition of mentoring and is clearly more reliable for making meaningful progress than any management "style" or strategy I have ever heard of. This concept succeeds even when it fails. To wit: if the person in question won't work diligently towards his own goals he certainly will never work with any passion towards yours. This incontrovertible truth has helped me to be more decisive in getting rid of non-contributors. The implications of "working for people's goals" are formidable and require a great deal of the "T word" (trust).

We will discuss this idea further in following chapters. The most important thing to remember is this: once you can commit to working towards organizational objectives from the direction of your peoples goals first you can expect to be rewarded with both quality production and meaningful progress over the long term.

Trust in the Process of Growth

"Trust the process" has become my mantra during inexplicably difficult times in my business career. There are times when things just don't work out the way they are supposed to (that's the breakthrough sentence of this book). "Trusting the process" puts all of the bruises and creative struggling in context. If one truly trusts the process then everything counts. All the micro failures that make up a successful enterprise will have a symmetry to them that forms a textured backdrop to the impending, and frequently invisible, breakthroughs that make things finally work. Outcomes are either positive or negative. The results are either wins or lessons on how to get future wins. With patience and perspective, it is understood that *everything* moves the organization forward.

Managing teams is an obscenely complex process and can't always be measured quantitatively. In fact, if most of your meaningful progress is of the quantitative variety (in the numbers, rather than in the culture) then your real leap forward is probably quite a ways off. You just aren't looking the right direction. Look for the necessary failures. Super teams go on a seven-steps-forward four-steps-back rhythm. Paying attention to (and recognizing) meaningful failures is the easiest and best way we have to make the necessary down-payment on our future successes.

Agreement

My business definition of agreement is "the recognition between people in an organization of parallel responsibilities to each other". Simply stated, a business relationship is as strong as the "agreement" between the people in it.

Agreement should allow for:

- Diversity of opinion
- Growth of both parties
- Successful failures
- Safe inter-directional communication
- Allowances for position safety
- The changing of ones mind

All of the above factors lead to true and powerful agreement between two people or two departments, divisions, etc. Given time they will take root and produce their fruit: High expectations!

Full Contact Leadership

"Full Contact" is the description I use to describe what I think what we should aspire to be in our leadership roles. Not pulling any punches, brave enough to work with the highest of expectations, willing to be fully honest and ethical in all of our dealing and knowing full well that we must start with ourselves. That is Full Contact Leadership.

One of the central aspects of effective leadership is the perception that the leader has of his or her self. A leader's self-perception will dictate much of what he chooses to do and say. This concept is worth examination because most leaders don't realize that their leadership persona is deliberate and can develop and change over time. Highly effective leaders actually see their jobs differently than less effective ones. Many leaders face career crisis when their idea of how they should act as a leader simply isn't working or is much less effective than they imagined it would be. Leaders who are new to their roles often simply act like another leader or manager who they have admired or envied. It is worth the effort to discover how your "boss" or "manager" picture originated. Here are a few questions to help you to get a handle on what your self-perception actually is:

- How do you see your self as a leader?
- Do you think the people you are leading see you in the same way?
- Do you feel like you need to "live up" to something or someone as a leader?

- Do you feel like it is a leaders job to collect power or to give it away?

- Does your leadership personality feel like an aid to you or a burden?

- Who serves whom in your organization?

- Did you act more "natural" before you were in a leadership role or after?

- Do you wish your team saw you in a different way?

- What would you change about your leadership persona in you could?

Levels of Leadership Self-Perception

One of the most important areas of your self-perception as a leader has to do with your relationship to the people you lead. How you see yourself in relation to your people says a lot about the kind of leader you are. This is also an area where highly developed leaders are distinctly different than their less-successful peers. The following graph shows how a leaders self-perception can evolve over time:

Self-Perception as Leader

When they first earn their way into a leadership role most people see themselves in the "I work for me" paradigm. They have had to compete for their position in most cases and are to looking out for themselves first and foremost. Frequently this newly minted manager actually sees his followers as a distraction or even as a burden. Typically, it does not take much time for his ego to kick in and for a rookie leader to test their new authority and power. This is the "my people work for me" stage and it can be very challenging for the followers, especially when the new leader has been promoted out of a group of former peers. Luckily, this leadership phase is usually brief.

There are leaders who spend entire careers as Stage Two authoritarian managers. You have probably worked for one or two of them in your career. The thoughtful leader will normally gradually ascend to level three. This is the "I work for my people" leader. He or she will take a very sympathetic stance with their people and will typically have trouble driving performance in their organization. This is especially true when the performance targets are top-down targets.

Ironically, the leader at this stage will typically feel like their people are dissatisfied with their situations despite the leader's interest and advocacy. In this stage leaders feel that they will get the best results managing from a peer approach, acting like their followers are friends or in a social situation that just happens to be a business. Of course the followers know better. The fact that the manager has a bigger office and makes more money is not lost on them. The manager in the "I work for my people" stage has not learned about leverage yet. They will realize that, just like with a mechanical lever, the closer you are to the subject or object the less ability you have to move it.

By far the most effective positioning as a leader is learned at Stage Four. This is the stage where the leader realizes that he actually works for his people's goals, and not for the people themselves. Obviously, this requires the leader to be in touch with his team's individual motives and goals and allows the leader to hold his people to a much higher standard for themselves. The leaders are not saying that the team must perform because he says so (Stage Two) or that he is at their service and will do anything he can to help them perform (Stage Three). The leader is saying that everyone is here to be successful and that it is his job to insure that it happens. This is an organization where people accomplish what they set out to accomplish and, in this way, the team as a whole performs at a very high level without any kind of manipulation or threat. Another way to state it is that the leader works for the organization's goals. Because an organization is just the sum total of many individuals, I prefer to see it as a leader working for the people's business goals and objectives.

The only catch is that the leader must really do her homework on her people, getting to know them and taking the time to learn what drives them as individuals (see The Myth of Motivation). When you study the best leaders and coaches, you will see stage four leadership in action. Most truly high performance teams are managed in this way. Where are you on the self-perception ladder? Is there room to improve? Take action and see how quickly the outside picture changes when the inside picture (self perception) changes first.

Soft Skills

Access to numerical information has been a real boon to modern corporations. Today's software allows us to slice and dice information and measurements in seconds in ways that would have taken weeks just a few years ago. For all of the advantages that this "instant information" has given us there are some drawbacks to as well. Because the information is so easy to get many of us have become "quant-jocks" using quantification and measurement as our primary means of gaining intelligence about our businesses. We use our numbers to make broad decisions about performance and strategy. We let our numbers draw conclusions for us about how things are really going.

In the past the accountants added everything up and translated the numbers for the executives. Today, because of the easy and immediate access to these business measurements, many executives have allowed themselves to become quantitative leaders rather that qualitative ones. Like anything that's easy, this focus on information is seductive and can allow managers and leaders to take short cuts in their decision-making, reducing or even eliminating the human element we used to rely on. People like to say that "the numbers don't lie" and that is certainly true, but they don't tell the whole truth either. They don't tell you everything you need to know about how a business or a department is doing. There are nuances that numbers and measurements can't see or discern. Things such as momentum, feel, commitment and morale is often hidden underneath our numerical measurements.

Marshall Goldsmith, a business leader and columnist with Fast Company magazine, makes his case for being a soft-side accountant:

"Given our addiction to measurement, and it's documented value, you would think that we would be more attuned to measuring the "soft-side" values in the workplace: how often we are rude to people, how often we are polite, how often we ask for input rather than shut people out, how often we bite out tongue rather than spit out a needlessly inflammatory remark. Soft values are hard to quantify but, in the area of interpersonal performance, they are as vital as any financial number. They demand our attention if we want to alter our behavior".

Marshall Goldsmith/FAST COMPANY—September 2003

Let's be respectful of all that the numbers can show us, and teach us, about our businesses. It would not be possible to run an effective business today without the kind of instant access we now have to our key numbers. The real-time measurements we now have access to allow us to hold ourselves, and our teams, accountable to results in an unprecedented way. This is a huge advantage. Let's also remember that the numbers are the lagging indicators for our businesses. The leading indicators are always at the staff and customer level and appear in people long before the numbers tell the story. Stay in touch with your soft skills, it's more important than ever.

Heavy Hands

One of the toughest leadership skills to learn is when to intervene in a situation and when not to. In fact, this sense of when to get involved is one of the best ways to truly distinguish between management and leadership. The manager is always involving himself in the details of the business. The manager believes that his intervening in small and large issues in his organization is always the right thing to do. A leader, on the other hand, is someone who has developed a particular kind of sensitivity to the issues and events that happen in his organization. He has learned that his intervention is not always going to be beneficial. He has learned to dismiss his own ego from the issue and think only in terms of what is best for his team. Clearly, there are times when leadership intervention in an issue is the only responsible course of action. There are other times when it is best to let the issue run it's course or let it be managed and resolved by the team, even if things get a little messy for a while.

There are risks that come from heavy managerial intervention and risks associated with managing with not enough intervention. Being a Full Contact Leader means knowing how to intelligently discern when intervention is necessary and when it is really not. Here are a few of the most common risks associated with both:

Risks that can come from Heavy Involvement:

- It can show a lack of confidence in your team's ability to resolve their own issues.

- You can build up an unnecessary dependence on your intervention.

- It can keep people on your team from developing resolution skills.

- Over time, you can create a team that functions much differently when you are there and when you are not.

- Managers who see themselves as referees tend to experience much more stress than necessary.

- Too many rules about how people relate to each other can cause people to forget that all they really need to do is be nice. You can't legislate "nice".

- Constant interventions can use up a lot of leadership time that could be spent on other (more valuable) pursuits.

Risks that can come from minimal involvement:

- Often issues take longer to resolve when the manager is not involved.

- Sometimes without the leaders involvement issues are resolved in the favor of the person with the biggest personality, not necessarily the person who is actually right.

- There is a risk that the team may mistake a light hand for the leader not caring about a certain issue or conflict.

It takes time for a leader to develop the sensitivity to know when intervention is necessary to resolve a situation in a fair and positive way. Over time your team will come to know intuitively which situations you are going to intervene in and which you will allow to take their natural course. You will build up a valuable kind of trust from your team when they know that your involvement in a situation means you consider it a serious issue and you are not just tangled up in it just to hear yourself talk.

Generally speaking, a leader should limit his involvement in issues that are not central to the objectives of the business. That certainly does not mean that the leader should not take a personal interest in his people. Non-business issues like intra-office relationships, personality clashes among team members and petty arguing between people should probably not be on your leadership radar screen.

Making a Difference from the Inside

Being a Full Contact Leader means knowing how to manage both down, across and up. We have focused most of our discussions on managing and leading the people you are responsible for. Obviously, your success as a leader depends mostly on your ability to get results through people. Other areas of leadership that need your attention and care are; leading and managing your peers and leading and managing your boss.

People take their reputations very seriously. This is especially true of very ambitious people. We work to build our reputation up and then we keep working to preserve and improve it as time goes on. It has been rightly said that our reputation is one of the only things we will get to keep from our work. The money will eventually be spent, the titles will come and go, even the people we get to work with and the important relationships we build will change over time. Our reputation, however, will stay with us.

We build our positive reputations by serving the needs of others. We have become valuable in our organizations by knowing important things and being able to do things well. Maybe you are one of those people who "gets things done" or you have the reputation of being very reliable, or highly creative, or you have a reputation for being accurately analytical, or for having a great sense of humor or perhaps you are technically proficient. Regardless of what your reputation actually is, you are known for something. That something is more valuable to you than any single job or working relationship you will ever have. What you are "known for" will eventually determine your income, title, responsibilities and job security. It's pretty important.

It is critical that we, as leaders, consider what we are known for. What would our peers say our reputation is? How about our bosses? Many companies are now doing 360-degree evaluations. When executed properly these evaluations can be very valuable. In a 360-degree evaluation you are evaluated by your subordinates (what a terrible word), your peers, and your superiors. This kind of evaluation can yield a total picture of a leader, with impressions of the subject coming from all angles. Frequently a leader will learn that the impressions people have of him vary wildly based on what his relationship is with the respondent. Positive changes can be made based on this kind of feedback.

What do we need to consider when we think about our reputations? I believe the most important thing a leader needs to understand is that a reputation is a decision. Over time we will decide what we are known for. Our reputations are actually a dynamic long-term construct of all that we say and do in our organizations. Once created, a leader's reputation can be very hard to change. So hard, in fact, that usually it is easier to actually change organizations than it is to change your reputation in the organization you are already in. That is one of the real upsides to changing a job; you get to decide what you are going to known for in your new environment.

Here are some questions to help you to get an accurate view of what your reputation in your organization really is:

- Under what circumstances are you sought out for input?

- Are you the recipient of a lot of gossip?

- Do people who are no longer with the your organization keep in touch with you?

- In what situations do you have the most fun?

- Are you being actively recruited by other companies in your field?

- Are you currently mentoring anyone?

- What is your compliment-to-criticism ratio when discussing your colleagues?

- Do your subordinates believe you have confidence in your bosses?

- Are there lots of people in your organization who you don't trust?

- Do you consistently take the time to offer thanks or congratulations to people outside of you department or region?

- How are you different than you were when you first joined your company?

- Are the people you feel closest to in your organization peers, subordinates or superiors?

- Do you frequently work on projects that are outside of your core responsibility?

Think about these questions. They will give you some insight in to what you are currently known for in your organization. Reputations are strange in that sometimes the only person who does not know their reputation in the person themselves. Your reputation is owned by you but affected by many others, this is why "reputation management" (to coin a phrase) is so complex. What follows are some reliable recommendations for taking control and actively improving your reputation. Recommendations:

- Get out of the gossip business. If you are currently on the receiving end of a lot of company gossip then you have cast yourself as a person who wants to hear it. Shut it down, this is not what you want to be known for.

- Actively seek out and introduce yourself to people in your organization who seem to be energetic and genuinely interested in doing well.

- Be careful about how interested you are in making certain that you get proper "credit" for things. It can be unseemly and accomplish just the opposite of what you actually want.

- Most leadership positions are based on managing routines. If you have a job where the same situations and issues arise over and over, don't keep using the same words and actions in your responses. Answer the question in a new way. Surprise people by taking a new and thoughtful tack in a situation. Reliability is good. Predictability is bad. It can be a fine line between them.

- Recognize reliable people inside and outside of your department for the consistently good job they do.

- When you have a new idea, make surprising progress on it before you take it up the ladder.

- Never bring up a problem that you have not taken the time to think through possible solutions for first.

- Be the person who recommends the next great business book or seminar.

- Volunteer for projects outside of what people perceive to be your area of expertise.

- Don't be the "Devil's advocate". It's a role preferred by people who have cynicism where their imaginations should be.

- Change up some of your routines for appearances sake.

- When you must fire someone, don't communicate the news with any kind of bravado or unnecessary explanation. There is nothing macho about someone on your team failing.

- Support a peer who is in the right even if his position is not popular.

- Be the person who is not always talking about how busy they are.

- Aggressively solve problems and see them through to the end.

Think of other actions that will help you be known in a way that you have decided and determined to be known. Some of these recommendations sound like they could have come straight from the Dale Carnegie business school, or at least I hope they do, we could all use more reminders what it really means to simply be nice, especially when we don't have to be.

Being a Full Contact Leader means not leaving your skill-set or your reputation to chance. Thinking in terms of what you want to be known for will help you develop into the leader you want to become.

Form Your Board of Directors

One of the personality traits that differentiate the Full Contact Leader is his or her openness to critique and contrary opinion. Having trustworthy confidantes to advise you is necessary to reaching your potential as a leader, especially in learning skills that do not come naturally to you. You will find that your ability to develop these kinds of relationships is in direct proportion to your ability to hear and accept what people have to say. We have all worked with those that say that they have trouble getting straight answers or quality feedback on issues. These are nearly always the same people who reflexively ignore or dismiss advice…sometimes even advice that they themselves have requested.

Most of the time, confidant relationships develop naturally between people who have learned to put their egos and prejudices aside when dealing with one another. In the course of a career these kinds of relationships usually turn out to be what is both most impactful at a certain job and the most rewarding. Full Contact Leaders formalize this process to ensure that they gain the most possible knowledge from confidant relationships. The formality and structure is accomplished by actually organizing a Board of Directors for your self as a person, as a professional, as a learning leader.

Think about the role of a board of directors for a corporation. Board members are chosen most often based on the wisdom, energy and experience they can bring to a growing business. In assembling a solid board of directors young companies can gain a real edge in their development and growth. I have seen situations where start-up corporations were able to get investment capital primarily on the strength of their boards.

I believe that your career as a successful leader is important enough to support with a board of directors. Like any corporation, your B.O.D will change shape over time depending on what sort of advice and guidance you may need as you develop as a truly effective leader. I have given this advice on organizing a B.O.D. for several years and have seen dramatic results from people by simply taking this formal step towards getting access to more experience-tested wisdom.

How do you from your B.O.D.? First think what you want to accomplish and whom you may know who have accomplished some of these things. Consider people both in and out of your current organization. Think about mentors you have had in the past (both formal mentor relationships and informal ones). Is there a peer that seems to have figured out some of the things you are still working on? Who do you know that has had a really broad mix of experiences? Many times this kind of person can be uniquely impactful in a board scenario. Who do you know who is just really smart and able to discern things most people miss? Unlike a corporate board, your B.O.D. will probably never be in the same place at the same time. In fact, if it seems likely that they might, your board is not nearly diverse enough. Think also in terms of people who energize you with their intellect or their joie de vivre.

Here are the final criteria for board selection, once you have an exciting list of people to consider. Filter your list of possible board members through these four steps:

1. Do they expect me to succeed? (you don't want non-believers on your board)

2. Do they know things that I don't?

3. Are they successful in their own right? (Remember, success can mean a lot of things: balance, fun, money, personal development, entrepreneurial success, benevolence, etc.)

4. Will they give it to me straight?

5. Are they available to me?

Filtering your candidates though that list should narrow it down quite a bit. There is no magic number for your personal B.O.D. I would think that two of three would be too few and that twelve or fourteen would be too many. Really it comes down to what and who you need to help you grow into the kind of leader and person you really think you can be.

Once you have what you feel is an excellent group for your board of directors you will have to decide exactly how formal you want to be in each of these relationships. I have seen successful relationships where the introduction has been very formal with the person meeting with a potential board member to ask if they would be agreeable to serving. Once the expectations were explained, the board member agreed and was very flattered to have been asked. Some of the best board relationships are never actually discussed. Rather, they are just known to be. I have had several of these de facto board member relationships over the years (on both sides of the relationship) and they have proven very beneficial though they are less formal.

I strongly suggest that you don't leave the active pursuit of advice, experience and wisdom to chance. Form your board of directors as a matter of priority. This is a big step towards becoming a Full Contact Leader.

The Myth of Motivation

There is a myth that permeates many contemporary business organizations. Like any myth that is accepted as a truth, this myth is a significant barrier to understanding and growth. It has to do with the motivation of the individuals who work in organizations. This myth is worth discussing because it is partially responsible for the debilitating arrogance of many managers and supervisors in relation to their teams. The myth is this: that "management" is responsible for the daily motivation of the people who work in their organizations. That if the manager/leader is a good motivator, then the team will produce more and generally have better results. This belief is especially prevalent in sales management but can be found everywhere. As far as I can tell this particular conceit has existed as long as there have been "bosses" of any kind. The whole idea of motivation as a verb has not been questioned nearly enough in the modern study of what makes for effective management. The very idea of management motivating people is arrogant because it makes two errant assumptions;

1. That the employees don't have enough of their own motives to want to work successfully.

2. That individual performance is best affected by manipulation, intervention or charismatic oratory by management.

The truth is that everyone has motives, or reasons, to work. And it is true that some people's motives will make them much more valuable to your company than other people's. It's OK to admit that there are people who come to work just to collect their paycheck with the least possible work or involvement. To believe that there are people whose motives are shallow does not make you cynical. There are such people and to not want them on your team makes perfect sense. What *is* cynical is to believe that without your motivation that the majority of your team (or company) would not do their best, or worse, that they would do as little as possible to stay on the payroll.

The traditional motivational model is, at its core, cynical and has not changed substantially since the 1950's. At its foundation, the motivational model of management depends on a gross underestimation of people's capabilities. It is this underestimation that makes "motivation" necessary. This message can be seen clearly in the motivational posters we have in our halls in the slogans we use to fire up the troops and heard in voices of our most "inspirational" leaders. Isn't it time to admit that these types of hackneyed shorthand get-some-boost-without-actually-training-new-skills tactics are the worst kind of manipulation? Would you like to estimate the number of meetings, seminars and conferences that have been complete wastes of time and money because of this approach to "motivation"? In many companies the executives themselves don't even bother to do the motivational talk themselves. They find an exciting hired gun and tell him to jack up the room.

How many executives have been befuddled by the fact that they got no real lift by having Mr. You-Can-Do-It give his best meeting-closing speech? As I mentioned before, sales managers and sales executives are the guiltiest by far. There has been a huge industry built around sales managers insatiable lust for the newest motivational fuel for their teams. Why are we so attached to this concept of motivation? When we have collectively become so much smarter about compensation, positive reinforcement, key business measurements, the study and understanding of personality traits, successful selling behavior and helpful technologies…why do we still cling to four-generations-old ideas about how to help our people perform better? I believe there are five answers to that question:

1. These ideas about motivation allow managers to "lead" without personal risk. If their motivational techniques seem to succeed, then all glory (and credit) goes to them. They successfully sparked the team, at least for the short term. Conversely, if the managers team does not respond to her motivational efforts it very easy to blame them. How many times have you heard a manager talk down about his people because they did not sufficiently respond to his fiery exhortations? In these situations the manager has no accountability to the outcomes, just the glory if it "works" and the right to be critical of his people if it doesn't.

2. It is cheap. Real training and skill-improvement initiatives are expensive. They require talented trainers who really know the day-to-day business issues (which many executive-level managers do not). Real training demands real preparation and forethought. Traditional motivational techniques can be executed without this level of planning and can usually be delivered with much less expense or preparation.

3. It is scalable. You can do a motivational speech or seminar in front of 10 or 10,000 people and basically say or do the same things. Sometimes having larger groups can even make the event seem more substantial and powerful. Traditional one-way motivating is conceived as a broadcast. You do not have to know the individuals or even the collective needs of the group. You do not need to worry about actual skill gaps that might exist in your people. You only need to motivate.

4. It is ego gratifying. What is more stimulating to a leaders self-image than the idea of standing behind a podium with their fist in the air inspiring their team to ever-greater heights. We grew up and became managers, not rock stars or professional athletes. Speechifying gives us our chance at that long-awaited standing ovation.

5. It appears to work sometimes. Occasionally a motivational event (a conference or a particularly moving speech) can really rouse people. It can be magical and make people feel the way they can feel with powerful music or an inspiring film. We have all been so inspired. We have been so pumped up that we wanted to kick down the doors of the conference room as we left. The question remains, however, are people really going to be better and more productive or are they just excited?

I believe the most useful way to think about motivation is to consider what you are really trying to do. Are you looking for actual business improvements? Is the goal to have an outcome that you can measure? If so, then you need to really reconsider how you perceive the process of improving a team. Everyone has motives. Everyone, including you and me, have reasons for the things they do and don't do. The very best way to help people improve is to get out of the motivation business and begin the real work of learning how to find the genuine motives that are already in your people. This process will be addressed in several different ways on these pages and in other quality books and articles. Let's look at a few of the most effective means of illuminating and addressing the success motives in your people.

It All Starts with Reasons

There are many short-term ways of getting people to do things they would not ordinarily do; contests, incentives, threats, embarrassment, etc. Even when these methods are initiated with care and good intentions they are all, at their roots, forms of manipulation. Manipulating someone is not necessarily a negative thing; we are all manipulated every day. The problem comes when we try to create long term change or improvement using short-term strategies like contests, incentives, threats, etc. A person must truly connect with his or her own core motives to be a top performer. Here is where you come in; a leader can play a key role in this connection process. This kind of help is one of the very few direct ways to affect and possibly influence the long-term level of motivation that an individual can bring to your team.

Here is my theory of motivation: Everyone walks around with two lists in their head. Some are more aware of the lists than others, but we all have them. One list is called "Reasons to Succeed". It is the list that has all of the good things that comes from financial and career success. It is the list of important things that a person can have, do, see, give, be, buy, etc. That list of all of those things that can become possible with success at work. The other list is called "what I will let get in my way". This is a list comprised mostly of circumstances, conditions and excuses. These are reasons why not. Everyone is pretty aware of what is on this list. Many people like to share this list as a way of explaining why they may not be accomplishing the things that are on their first mental list. There are probably a few people in your life who like to share this list…a lot. I have met people for whom sharing this kind of list is nearly a full-time job. A further discussion of these lists is in the chapter on Developing A High Performance Team.

The Full Contact Leader knows that his job is to help connect people to their motives for doing well. There are many reasons why a person may not be motivated to do well in your organization. Ninety-nine percent of these reasons are inside of their own head. They may have low self-esteem. They may have a very short time perspective. They may have destructive or distracting habits. They may just not know how to work successfully. This kind of list would never be complete. There are as many kinds of performance issues as there are different kinds of people. Just think about how complex your own motives can be. Your best bet is always going to be speaking honestly to your people and really getting to know them. Most performance gaps are best addressed at the personal motivation level and are not rooted in knowledge or technical gaps. Everyone on your team has very good reasons to do well and succeed at their role in your organization. Every one of them wants to perform at a high level and be recognized for that performance. As a leader, it is your job to find the "why" in every individual you are responsible to.

How vs. Why

Traditional management techniques are overwhelmingly aimed at the "how" part of the job performance equation. We typically think in terms of what we can teach our people that will help them to perform better. It is proper and necessary to think in terms of "how" but to get maximum performance from people leaders need to get into the "why" business.

Everyone who works where you work has a reason to be there. These reasons (motives) to work are wildly varied and individual. Understanding people's "why's" is one of the keys to effectively leading them. The "why" is the bottom-line reason why a person gets up and comes to work in the morning. It a person doesn't have a "why" they won't get up and come to work in the morning. A huge step in high-performance leadership comes from beginning to find out why the people on your team work. The "why" part of the motivation equation is where all of the real motive energy comes from in people. Think about yourself for a moment. You know what your "why" is and you know that the motive force that comes from it has been responsible for all of your professional accomplishments. Everyone has his or her own reasons for working and succeeding. Knowing their motives, goals and hopes for their jobs will help you connect with your people in a way that simply teaching another new technique could never accomplish.

It should also be noted that in our careers as leaders we will all have people on our teams who do not have motives (why's) in their lives that are substantial enough to make them a valuable part of our teams. It is not any kind of value judgment; it is just a simple fact. If someone's motivation for coming to work is to be able to afford a case of beer and dinner on Friday night then they will probably not spend much time in your boardroom. No amount of motivational speeches will change him because speeches won't change his "why".

Traditional charismatic motivation has a place in business but it is not going to yield sustainable progress or growth in people. Real business results are only going to come from doing the hard work of discovering the motives of your people.

- Why they come to work?

- What they hope to accomplish?

- Who is depending on them?

- How do they see themselves in the future?

• What they hope to become?

• What do they need to learn to reach their potential?

Once you know your people's "why's" you can get to work on training skills (how's) and then shaping opportunities around those motives. In this way you can truly provide a place where people can find their own greatness and make their maximum value contribution to your organizational goals.

Developing A High Performance Team (One Person at a Time)

One of the skills that differentiate a leader from a manager is the ability to develop people. Leaders are able to help people become bigger and more capable. Think back on your career. Consider the bosses you worked with that had the biggest impact on you. You have probably had one or two who actually empowered you to change who you were. They helped you to grow your capabilities and expectations and, because of that growth, allowed you to open up a whole new world of possibilities. That is what real leaders do.

Before the serious work of developing a high-performance team can begin we must acknowledge an important point; teambuilding is a process, not an event. Great teams come together over time and form in both predictable and unpredictable ways. All great teams share some traits in common (see the chapters on Trust and Atmosphere). The only reliable way to construct a truly excellent team is to focus on developing one person at a time.

Six Truths about Developing People

1. Our purpose as leaders is to have a positive impact on our marketplace, to provide a meaningful service or a valuable product.

2. Developing a high-performance team is our means to that purpose.

3. You develop a team one person at a time.

4. People are different.

5. Every person has potential.

6. With our people we have two primary responsibilities;

   • To make them aware of their own potential.

   • To help them achieve it.

Driving Performance with Your Team

High performance always starts with high expectations. The leaders job is to have his high expectations in place before a new person even joins the organization. These high expectations are like the furniture; they are there before the people show up. A leader's performance expectations must be communicated in a positive and non-threatening way. Discussions and meetings must all be anchored by some planned dialogue about "here's what we are here to do" or "let's review what the target looks like". The leader would be better off making the mistake of talking about his expectations too much than too little. If the leader has done her job communicating team expectations you should see reminders everywhere you look and everyone from the receptionist to the V-P knows exactly what we are going to do as a team and where they fit in to the picture. These ardently communicated expectations form the context for all of the preparation and training that is going to happen with the team. To train new skills or techniques without an expectations context is a mistake that a lot of managers make. Make sure your people know that they are learning *this* so that they can then go accomplish *that*.

Train for Success

Once the proper expectations have been set, serious people development can begin. This is an area many leaders differ in their approach. One aspect that most will agree on is that you must always start with the end in mind; what do these people need to know how to do? How do we go about teaching it? How then do we measure the effectiveness of our teaching? These are questions that should be considered before organizing any people-development efforts. One of the most common mistakes made in teaching people new things is an over-emphasis on "educating" people on the subject at hand. Professional trainers are some of the worst offenders. Money is spent, people show up, the session is executed, people are taught stuff and then they go home. Now they know something new, but is that really the goal? Not necessarily. Most conventional training is not really "training" at all, it is educating. It is modeled after the classrooms we all spent 13-plus years in. That type of environment is geared toward teaching and not necessarily training. If your expectation as a leader is that the people you are training are supposed to go *DO* something different or better after the sessions then this traditional model may not be what you want. Here is how it works:

Education <Results In> Knowledge

Training <Results In> **Action!**

The real purpose of our training is not that they *know*, it's to prepare them to DO. So what we need to think about when setting up training sessions are the following:

- What do they need to know how to DO?
- How do we best get them ready to DO?

- How can we set up practice scenarios in our training that will show them how to DO?

- How can we measure their readiness to go DO?

Thinking in this way about training helps your people contribute their new skills to the organization much more quickly. Take some time to review your training programs and make sure they are yielding the actions you want rather than simply the knowledge.

Helping People Develop into High Performers

Over time all leaders realize that not everyone is meant to be successful in one place. Sometimes it is a timing thing, sometimes there is a mismatch of a certain person's personality and the personality of the organization they are a part of. Every leader has stories of people they were very highly impressed by who fell flat on their face when they joined their team. We all have the opposite story as well; of the person we had very little excitement about when they joined the team who went on to make a huge impact. Remembering all of those stories is important because they illuminate what an inexact science people development can be. As leaders, we must learn development skills that will be reliable for us with many different kinds of people. There are leaders who can only work and succeed with one kind of person on their team; many times that person is very much like the leader himself. This kind of leader will never be able to compete with someone who knows how to work and succeed with many differing people and personalities.

Jim Rohn, the well-known speaker and trainer, has said that the best way to get results with people is to "meet them where they are". This means learning why they are a part of your organization (see The Myth of Motivation chapter) and what they are trying to accomplish there. The best leaders know how to learn what drives their people and add that to the overall context of what they are trying to do as a department or a business. A successful organization works like a quilt. Everyone is sewing his or her little patch into the larger whole. By itself nobodies little patch is very impressive. When all sewn together it can be beautiful. The leaders job is to decide what the whole quilt will look like when it is complete.

To learn how big of a piece of the whole (quilt) any one person can contribute the leader must learn what drives them. As referenced before, I like to imagine that everyone has two lists that they carry around in their head all the time. The first list is called "what I want" and it contains all of the person's hopes, goals, dreams and desires. All of the big and little things this person wants. The second list is called "what I will get in my way". It contains all of the distractions, perceived roadblocks, internal and external challenges and circumstances that may conspire to keep the person from getting all that they want. The most highly motivated among us have a very short "what I will let get in my way" list and a very long "what I want" list. That is another way to look at ambition isn't it? Here is what these two lists might look like for a normal person we bring in to our organization:

What I Want	What I Will Let Get in My Way
To make a lot of $	My spouse is not supportive
To do "important" work	I can be very moody
To move up the company ladder	I like to sleep in in the morning
To put my kids through college	I don't think long term
For my family to see me as successful	I have trouble learning new things
To retire to the beach	I am basically lazy
A new car	
To start a charitable foundation	
To be able to take care of my parents	

To develop people it helps to know what they have on their "what I want" list. These are their reasons to succeed. These are the reasons why they could have a big impact on your organization. It is incumbent on the leader to learn what these motivators are in people. In many cases, a good leader can actually add things to a person's mental "what they want" list. Possibilities and opportunities that the person did not even know were available to them. Items on the "what I will let get in my way" list are typically going to either be disruptive traits, bad habits or external circumstances that have a negative influence on the person and their ability meet their real potential on your team. Leaders usually can't do much about these issues. In most cases the leader can help a person the most by keeping them focused on the first list; what they want to accomplish. To put it very simply, a person will be a consistent performer to the extent that their first mental list is longer than the second. Over time we will all work with people who cannot make any meaningful contribution to the team because they just have too many things they will let distract them and get in their way. You will work with people during your career who really don't want to succeed. That is an inevitability and part of the process of developing a team.

Managing Performance

The most important skill for managing performance is positive reinforcement. The old cliché of "catching people doing it right" is dead on. In another chapter we discuss "success events" and how important it is for leadership to learn how to recognize and reinforce the three distinct types of successful behavior in their people. It is always easier to reinforce correct behavior than it is to address unsuccessful behavior or ineffective performance. The reasoning for this is simple; people want to hear positive reinforcement, so they listen. It is much harder to provide effective coaching by bring attention to negative outcomes and trying to correct from there. That is why you need a reliable strategic approach to coach performance improvements.

Managing Deviations

The first step in learning how to manage for improvement is to know what to work on and what not to. For our purposes, let's call unsuccessful behaviors "deviations". It does not mean that the person who is not performing is a deviant it just means that what they are doing (or how they are doing it) is not working and is a deviation from what will actually work.

In the world of sales we are taught to discern in a closing situation whether an issue with a prospect is an "objection" or a "condition". It is important to know because if you proceed without knowing you can waste a lot of time and get very frustrated. An objection is something that can be handled on the spot. Many times objections are just a gap in understanding on the part of the prospect. Perhaps the salesperson did not explain something clearly. In any case, objections can be worked through to a successful conclusion. Conditions, on the other hand, are true obstacles that will prevent a successful outcome. A condition might be that you are in front of the wrong person, or that the company you are speaking with has no real need for what you are selling. There is no amount of selling skill that can overcome a condition.

The difference between an objection and a condition is a key learning for a professional salesperson. In leadership there is a similar fork in the road when it comes to knowing whether you can truly manage a person through a performance issue. It has to do with the difference between "habits" and "character traits". Like objections, habits can be changed and, with effort, worked through towards a successful outcome. Character traits are a whole other matter. Like sales conditions, character traits are what they are. They cannot be altered by the leader, even if that leader is very persistent and has the best possible intentions. To use computer language; habits are programmable and can be altered. Character traits are on the hard-drive.

If I had learned the difference between habits and character traits earlier in my career I would have far fewer gray hairs now. Understand that no matter how skilled you are as a leader you will not be able to alter someone's basic character. The first step in managing for improvement is to decide whether the issue is a simple habit or a character trait of the person in question. If it is a character trait that is preventing the person from performing to an acceptable level there is no training or development recourse.

The three keys to managing successful performance are:

- Recognizing Success Events.
- Expecting the right things to be done.
- Noticing and taking positive action when they are not.

We have to catch them doing it right AND catch them doing it wrong to truly affect performance. How long should we let someone do something we know will not work? As leaders, we must take advantage of teaching and partnering opportunities. How else are we going to show our people them that we care about how they do and actually expect them to be an important part of our team?

Top leaders and managers develop a keen sense of "deviations". As we discussed before, these are habits, attitudes and activities than will not result in success. I am sure you can think of 100 examples from your business. For my first 5 years in management the only performance discussion techniques I had ever heard was the classic "sandwich" method. That is where you compliment the person, then do your critique and then follow up with another compliment. I am not sure I have ever seen the sandwich method work, even though it has been taught to managers for 1,000 years. At best, the method works only to let the person know that the manager is aware of the problem. At worst it is manipulation and a waste of time.

As leaders who actually want to help our people improve we will need to learn coaching techniques that will yield change and improvement. We need reliable ways of communicating issues to our people. Remember, in high performance environments there are actually more performance issues to address because everyone is expected to perform at a higher level. What follows is a five-step process for coaching people positively through performance issues. This is a highly effective approach that has been used successfully for decades in business, coaching and teaching. It should be done as a private meeting and should last no more than 10 minutes. The objectives are to identify a performance issue, decide on a solution to fix the issue, agree on follow up and confirm the plan for successfully resolving the problem. Here are the five steps with their associated descriptions:

1. Identify it.

Tell the person what the deviation is. I don't recommend using the word "deviation" in this conversation. You would simply say something like "I have noticed that you have been turning in your payroll reports very late". You simply state the issue to get it out in the open. In most cases the person has been wondering if an issue is going to be addressed or if you (the leader) have noticed the problem.

2. Say why it concerns you.

"This issue concerns me because…". You tell the person exactly why the performance shortfall is an issue.

3. Relate back to their goals and potential.

Here is where it really helps to know your people. Knowing what their goals and motivations are allows you to address the performance issue in the context of their career, not simply as counter to the needs of the business. "This issue is of particular concern because I know that it is your goal to become the supervisor of the payroll department. I am sure you can understand why it would be especially important for a person who wants to be a leader to be very reliable. As a supervisor, you will need to model the kind of behavior you expect from your team".

4. Come to an agreement/solution to change the behavior.

Here is where the person themselves gets involved in fixing the situation. "Janet, what do we need to do about this issue?" You let the person come up with his or her own solution to the performance issue. Sometimes it helps to confirm with a simple "will that work?" question. You then ask if there is anything you as the leader can do to help in this change or improvement.

5. Solidify agreement and affirm your support and belief.

Confirm the plan and your agreement together. "OK Janet, as I understand our plan, going forward you are going to gather all of the branch reports you need the day before payroll reports are due. That will allow you to have plenty of time to finishing before they are actually due. Does that sound right? For the next month I want you to tell Marty when you have all of the branch reports collected. That way I will know that your plan is working well. OK? That sounds great Janet. Thanks for your interest in solving this problem. Let's get back to work."

This sequence must be practiced. It should never sound like manipulation. Take a few minutes and think through one of your repeating performance issues. It helps to visualize a real person and how the dialogue might fit them. Take it through the steps and imagine how the conversation would go. In this sequence you never asked why the work was not being done right in the first place. I have seen this dialogue work well with every kind of performance issue. Make sure that you sound like yourself and not a robot repeating a technique. Use your own words and mannerisms and you will be and sound natural and authentic.

As long as the issue is a just a bad habit and not a character trait this technique will work. Any plan is better no plan and these five steps will give any leader an organized script to help them arrive at the resolution they need. This technique is a positive way to confront a performance issue with someone that you care about and want to do well (which are the only people you should have on your team anyway).

The Competency Ladder

One of the challenges that leaders face in developing a high-performance team is figuring out successful ways to teach and train new and improved skills to their team members. Every era of business writers that I have ever read have had at least one thing in common; they consider their time to be a time of especially significant volatility and change. You can read about the accelerating pace of change and innovation in books written in the 1940's, 50's, 60's and all the way to the most contemporary and forward-thinking business books of today. It is fair to say that the ability to understand how people can learn and retain new skills and understandings has always been, and will always be, a key trait of the most successful leaders.

The "competency ladder" is an interesting phenomenon because of three unique characteristics.

1. It has been referred to in many important books and academic studies going way back to the 1960's and 1970's.

2. I have seen the basic concept referred to by more than a dozen different names.

3. No one seems to know the origin of the concept. In my own research I have found many claims of original authorship of the model, mostly from the worlds of academia and psychology, but never a confirmed originator.

The usefulness of the model is in how it can help a leader understand exactly where a person is in the process of learning something. By knowing this, a successful leader can help her people advance their skills and understandings much quicker than in traditional repetition and/or study techniques. The model can help keep you from spinning your wheels working on something with someone who is not going to "get" it no matter what is said or done (see: The Can't/Won't Crossroads chapter for more information on this topic). The language is a little complex but the concepts are simple and helpful. What follows are the generally accepted descriptions of the different levels on the competency ladder.

The Competency Ladder

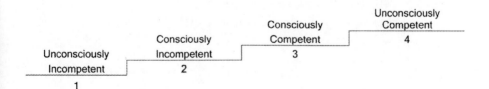

1—Unconscious Incompetence

- The person is not aware of the existence or relevance of the skill area.

- They don't know that they don't know.

- The person is not aware that they have a particular deficiency in the area concerned.

- The person might deny the relevance or usefulness of the new skill.

- The person must become conscious of their incompetence before development of the new skill or learning can begin.

- The aim of the trainee or learner and the trainer or leader is to move the person into the 'conscious competence' stage, by demonstrating the skill or ability and the benefit that it will bring to the person's effectiveness.

2—Conscious Incompetence

- This step sounds bad but it is actually significant progress from level one.

- The person becomes aware of the existence and relevance of the skill.

- The person is therefore also aware of their deficiency in this area, ideally by attempting or trying to use the skill.

- The person realizes that by improving their skill or ability in this area their effectiveness will improve (they have a motive reason to learn it).

- Ideally the person has a measure of the extent of their deficiency in the relevant skill, and a measure of what level of skill is required for their own competence.

- The person ideally makes a commitment to learn and practice the new skill, and to move to the 'conscious competence' stage.

3—Conscious Competence

- The person achieves 'conscious competence' in a skill when they can perform it reliably at will.

- The person will need to concentrate and think in order to perform the skill.

- The person can perform the skill without assistance.

- The person will not reliably perform the skill unless thinking about it—the skill is not yet "second nature" or "automatic".

- The person should be able to demonstrate the skill to another, and is usually the best possible teacher for others.

- The person should ideally continue to practice the new skill and, if appropriate, commit to becoming 'unconsciously competent' at the new skill.

- Practice is the single most effective way to move from stage 3 to 4.

4—Unconscious Competence

- The skill becomes so practiced that it enters the unconscious parts of the brain—it becomes "second nature".

- Common examples to use for analogies are driving, sports activities, typing, manual dexterity tasks, listening and communicating.

- It becomes possible for certain skills to be performed while doing something else or "multitasking", for example, knitting while reading a book, driving while talking on the phone, etc.

- The person might now be able to teach others the skill, although after some time of being unconsciously competent the person might actually have difficulty in explaining exactly how they do it—the skill has become largely instinctual.

- This arguably gives rise to the need for long-standing unconscious competence to be checked periodically against new standards.

This competency model can be very useful for a leader to really grasp and understand. The model can give a leader some important new vocabulary pieces to describe the process of getting better at something. For most people it is easier to see the ladder practically when thinking about a physical or technical skill. If you think about it for a while you can probably think of some skill (or lack of skill) where you yourself are on each of the distinct levels. You need to remember levels apply to people skills or "soft" skills just like they apply to technical or physical skills. Personally, I can remember being at the different levels in many of the areas where I have progressed and I can also remember how it feels to be stuck on a particular level and unable, because of a lack of practice or commitment, to improve. This feeling is commonly referred to as "golf".

One of the best uses for this model is in developing training programs. When you are organizing a training session or preparing a trainer these competency levels, and a working knowledge of how to move through them, can make all the difference in how effective a training program can be. One key understanding to have when you are setting up a training program is that a trainer who is at the level three, or consciously competent, will almost always be a better trainer than someone at level four. The "level three" practitioner has just learned the skill and is still have to consciously perform. Someone at level four, for whom the technique or skill is "second nature", will usually have much less success explaining or demonstrating something in a way a non-expert can understand.

An Alphabet of Characteristics found in High Performance Teams

A. There is a top down commitment to self-improvement.

B. People improve over time (they don't come at a certain level and stay there).

C. There are always new ideas being tested and evaluated.

D. There are examples of, and demonstrated enthusiasm for, lots of different careers (not just executive level leaders and performance leaders, but leaders of all kinds).

E. Everybody knows who the customer is.

F. The leader subscribes to the "praise in public, critique in private" model.

G. There is a competitive atmosphere.

H. The leader knows how to keep his business simple in his communications.

I. There is a deeply held belief that intelligent effort is always rewarded.

J. The meetings are highly participative and fun (they don't just exist on their own momentum).

K. Members of the team have "taken ownership" of the organization.

L. Everyone knows what they (as a team) are trying to accomplish.

M. Turnover happens faster (not slower) than in non-high performance offices.

N. There is value placed on diversity (it is understood that not everyone is the same or here for the same reasons).

O. The team celebrates wins together.

P. There are some consistent "cornerstone" traditions in the company, office or region.

Q. There are frequent contests and promotions for people at all levels.

R. The leader is clearly doing well in all important areas (life-balance wise, health, psychologically and ethically) and not just financially.

S. There is a clear and obvious team commitment to client service.

T. Good ideas are celebrated rewarded no matter where they come from.

U. There is a recognition that that everyone is not *supposed* to succeed (success is a decision that we all make individually and recognize as a group).

V. Office gossip is not rewarded with attention or participation.

W. The leader realizes that what they really have to manage is the environment. He knows that the office atmosphere can actually compel success or prevent it.

X. The leader understands that momentum is a decision.

Y. The leader has realized that some people need a "boss" figure in their careers and some don't.

Z. The leader encourages every person on his or her team to think like a business…as an entrepreneur.

Atmosphere

The ability to create and sustain a positive high performance atmosphere within an organization is the master skill of professional management. It is so important and elusive that most business literature dedicated to the topic is written from a point of view that leaves most of us feeling that the ability to create a truly inspired workplace is reserved for preachers, mystics and generals. In my own studies I have found almost no practical advice on creating a high performance environment or atmosphere in our organizations. Yet everyone agrees that this ability is a, or perhaps "the", major component necessary for truly exceptional achievement in a team effort over the long term. Why are these skills mystified in this way? Can they be so elusive and unlearnable that we must use this visionary/voodoo imagery to describe them?

Most of the examples of great business leaders we hear about describe these inspired men (they are all men) as being able to create a mission or campaign that is so compellingly irresistible that people are motivated to superhuman efforts to insure a favorable, if not legendary, outcome. As the stories go, a leader struck in the Lombardi/Iacocca/Churchill/Welch mold arrives with a seemingly impossible mandate or vision in mind. The followers, who are struck instantaneously by his vision and charisma, fall in line to passionately pursue the grail of choice. The whole picture is nothing more than hog wash. The movie star luster associated with CEO's in the 80's and 90's has worn off and it's a good thing. Most of us have too much important work to do to wait for General Patton to show up. I have nothing whatsoever against visionaries or zealots, but there is a rather fundamental problem with their getting all of the credit for exceptional results that were created through the committed efforts of others. Most "idea people" I know do not have much of an appetite (or aptitude) for the activities that will be required to move their idea to a fruitful outcome. On the other side of the coin, many "implementers" do not spring forth tons of break-through ideas. One is no good without the other. Is it possible that we have made significant leaps less likely by perpetrating this mythology about our "idea people"? I imagine that many of the true visionaries have gone unrecognized because there were not enough skilled and motivated "workers" around to make things happen. The difference is in the doing. Why don't we allow most of the glory for the implement-ers? There certainly is no glory without them.

Creating a highly-charged super-expectant atmosphere of achievement is not magic, it is effort. Creating a place where people can come to be excellent requires that we believe that people can and will perform mir-acles if we will get out of their way and spare them the Gipper stories. We have legends in the making right now. We simply don't need the old ones anymore.

Let's see if we can distill some of the more learnable nuances of creating this ideal of a high energy, high performance, change-ready business atmosphere. It will be necessary to break things down into much smaller pieces to create a recipe that is both implementable and under-standable by leaders with diverse personality types in broadly differing situations.

This high performance environment we seek is the sum total of all the factors in an organization relating to it's culture. It is the combination of history, training, personality, bureaucracy, ethics, compensation, energy, organizational objectives and access to information. I believe that this dizzying array of variables to consider has made the creation of a great atmosphere a seemingly unattainable part of teambuilding. To add to the confusion, we know that there are people who can manipulate and understand these myriad factors naturally and with almost no effort. I am not one of these people so I have had to take great pains to learn this skill like I have learned others; through mistakes and the regret associated with doing it wrong. Here's what I've figured out:

The most useful way to think about office/team atmosphere is as "expectation management". The people that succeed in creating and sustaining an excellent, fertile atmosphere are expert expectation managers. (They are extremely sensitive to what their team believes outcomes will be in many different areas.) People who work with these leaders simply define "good work" differently than those who work for average or unenlightened managers. To help us get a better grip on this highly intangible concept I want to review what atmosphere is and isn't.

What it is:

- It is the "personality" of your organization.

- It's what people miss when they are away.

- A great atmosphere in an office does not necessarily cause great things to happen, rather, it _lets_ great things happen.

- The atmosphere sets the "speed limit" for your team. Because it is both a *creator of* and a *result of* expectations no organization can, for the long-term, rise higher than it's atmosphere will allow.

- Atmosphere is vibratory; it is there even when you and your team are not.

What it isn't:

- It isn't measurable, yet it controls everything.

- It isn't in your Mission Statement.

- It cannot be mandated

- It isn't physical, but it has a life of it's own.

- It isn't in your Manager's Training Manual.

Creating a positive powerful atmosphere in your organization will require a great deal of planning and effort. You will need a strategy for growing it. Once it is established, it will run on it's own momentum. Remember that atmosphere cannot be altered directly. It's not the result of a campaign, a slogan or an initiative. *It is the effect of many causes.* It is fragile, but it will take on a life of it's own if attended to properly.

What follows is the best formula or recipe that I can imagine for creating a highly productive and perceptibly enjoyable team atmosphere in your organization.

Nice People	E	
Common Values	Q	A
High Expectations	U	VIBRANT
Requisite Skills	A	DYNAMIC
Authentic Leadership	L	ATMOSPHERE
Challenging Objectives	S	

I am hopeful that this recipe does not need much explaining. You will notice that most of the above comes pretty easily, even naturally. The vast majority of people are nice. They have a grounding set of values and would prefer to be in a successful outfit. What needs attention in most organizations are the bottom three requisites, the ones that come from management. It is worth noting again that a manager/leader is solely responsible for her office's atmosphere. She must be extremely, even obsessively, attendant to the meaningful details that go together to create this rare business environment. I really believe that the office atmosphere is more reliable than a CAT scan when it comes to reflecting what's going on in the head of a would-be leader or manager. Your office's "feel" is a direct reflection of your (the manager's) beliefs. Do you think that business teamwork can be fun? Do you believe that your team can accomplish unique things? Can you say, "Thank God it's Monday"? Are you willing to be emotionally vulnerable to create an atmosphere of trust? Do you like your people? Can you handle not getting every bit of the credit that comes with a job well done? If the answer to these questions is yes (or at least maybe) then we are ready to move on to discussing some actual steps to creating your own atmosphere of excellence in your organization or office.

Steps to Creating an Atmosphere of Excellence

A. Realize who is in control and work on that person first.

Any team environment is a reflection of the leader. Stale and monotonous, inspiring or volatile, cranky or fickle, it can be said that the atmosphere of the department or office is always exactly as its leader wants it to be. This is true because of the parallels between the personality of the leader and the personality of the organization. This is why quick fixes like mission statements (without the proper grounding), corporate outings, and short-term campaigns can't really work. They are at their roots at odds with the leaders comfort zone and "way of getting things done". Until a learning leader/manager is ready to improve and change on a fundamental level, his staff cannot respond in a meaningful way. This is why most really speedy turnarounds take place only when a new leader shows up. This is an unfortunate reality of business (and team sports) because when it happens a number of erroneous conclusions are drawn. The new (imported) leader then gets way too much credit for firing-up a team who would have been willing to perform at a higher level all the while, and the teams members feel like farm animals who have finally been prodded in the right direction.

When the current manager is authentic in her enthusiasm or really turned on by a new idea or opportunity the team will respond quickly and with vigor. They know this leader and can sense her actual excitement stemming from a new understanding or initiative. These facts put the present manager in an excellent position for real renewal and improvement in the team environment. A warning: Spend your enthusiasm and passion conservatively. Look for things to get excited about but don't jump on every bandwagon, even when you are expected to. Your credibility with your team is priceless and will be the foundation of all the great things that you accomplish together today and tomorrow. Apathy can settle in quickly when a leader has a new passion monthly and is constantly "reinventing" and "paradigm shifting". Suggestion: Avoid any new ideas that sound really easy, anything that you can't explain using real words or anything that you have read about in the last 48 hours. Remember, the guy who is most likely to roll his eyes at a new idea thinks that "paradigms" are worth about twenty cents (get it?). He's the one who has to get on board or at least have the energy to get out of the way when everybody else does.

B. Get the Picture!

Everything substantial is created twice: Mentally and then physically. A great team atmosphere will not happen accidentally. You must have a guiding vision or you, and subsequently your team, will be affected, distracted and altered by everything that happens out of the ordinary. This vision, or mind-picture, of what kind of environment you are working towards will be very useful for comparison to your current reality. It will also allow you to act and make decisions that parallel and seem to fit what you are working towards. A great team environment is always a "work in progress" but it does develop it's own momentum and can be a very comforting thing especially in times of flux. A positive, energized high-octane office environment will sustain progress through times of change and uncertainty. This being true, the leader must be resolute in not letting temporary things interfere with the general positive flow of the team atmosphere or his personal atmosphere. Things like low sales, new people, heavy or intimidating competition, change in personnel, disappointing outcomes, new policies, personal problems and negative influences from above can set things off track, or worse, cause a leader to lose touch with his objectives completely. The leader really does need a clear picture of the kind of environment he is trying to create. One of the reasons this is so important is that his team will watch very closely to see if this vision and enthusiasm with survive (and not dim) in the face of seismic events in the organization. Understanding this, an enlightened manager can really benefit from dramatic or unusual things happening around her because it gives her a chance to show (without having to say a thing) that her vision is sturdy and resilient. A strong and forward-thinking leader will benefit greatly when lightning strikes because it gives him a chance to demonstrate the power of a relentlessly positive and resolute atmosphere.

So the big question becomes: Are you willing to take the time and energy to *originate* a compelling vision for your team? This creative effort, once initiated and sustained, can be the breakthrough event for any organization. Here are some exercises to help you begin to piece together a picture of how you want your organization to be and feel:

Picture your ideal working environment. I recommend going to your office or shop at a non-work time when you can be alone, sit down and turn off all those fluorescent lights. Relax. Think about the most creative, energized, fun and challenging work place you can imagine.

What do you see? Why are the people so energized? Why are they happy to be here? How is this ideal the same or different from your current reality? Are you in the picture? What are you doing? Do you picture your current staff in this ideal vision or are the people strangers? You may have to sit for a while for your imagination to get rolling. Get yourself a cup of coffee or tea and relax. Your mind will have very strong ties that associate this place with the present and "how things have always been". The status quo is a very powerful adversary in this process and must be fought with diligence.

This process of "visioning" is only the first step. Now write down your ideas for this idealized workplace. Why would it be a great place to work? What is completely different about it? Why would people love to be a part of it? If you can, develop a name for this envisioned place. This can act as a label for your picture and give it handle for people to grasp onto when you start building towards it. Some of the names I've heard are: "SuccessLab", "Team 2006", The Akron Project", "GTB Skunkworks", "The Strike Force", "ExpiriTeam B", "The RTG Initiative" and "NexTeam". This name does not have to make any sense to anyone but you and your team. In fact, usually the best (and most fun) names come from team members.

C. Put it in Motion!

You must now become a rabid enthusiast about how things will be in your organization. This is the stage where the people on your team will decide if this is "for real" or not. You cannot use your idealized vision of your organization to downgrade people. Your team must not suffer through comparison to the new standard. This could leave people emotionally unattached to this new vision and with no real ownership of it. A better way to deal with incongruities is to have the person, or people, creatively explain how something could have been done differently, more in line with our vision or however you have come to know it. This is why the vision or objective must be concrete enough to be verbalized and described easily. You must make it a nearly full-time job to help everyone to understand his or her important role in this new and exciting reality.

These encounters should be mostly private and very participative. Watch people. Look closely for their hidden talents. When doing this, proceed with the idea that they may be doing the wrong job or assignment. Maybe they should be managers. Maybe they should not be on this team at all. You must cleanse your mind of all preconceptions. It is these biases, and people's innate desire to avoid change, that has very likely given rise to any stagnation or apathy that may have formally existed. Visualize people in different positions and using different skills. What is the most meaningful way that each of these talented people can be more important to the team? Why haven't they been impact makers before (if that is the case)? Think of REAL reasons why each person in your organization is critical to the mission. Ask them questions like:

- What is your most unused talent?

- In what areas do you feel the ability to lead?

- What would make it more fun to come to work?

- What part of your job do you look forward to least?

- What's your specialty?

- What about this organization do you miss when you are away?

- What would you like to be known for in the organization?

- If you were to leave this team, what would you do career-wise?

- Who on our team is missed the most when they are gone?

- What is something we do around here that has never made sense to you?

- Among your peers, who would say is the most influential?

- Who do you see asserting themselves as a leader in the office?

- What would be the first change you would make if it were your decision alone?

After you have these informal, but critical, interviews you will begin to discover some important things about your people and their perception of their jobs, their peers, and their sense of "self" within the organization. Notes:

1. Do not organize these talks by appointment or all in one day or week. The key to getting meaningful insights is a casual approach, as free from structure as possible.

2. Do not ask questions that will allow a person to say negative things about a teammate. This would hurt the credibility of the process. Also, that's what people have (sadly) come to expect from management, so refraining from this kind of gossipy questioning will be a fresh and different approach (which is nearly the whole point).

3. Throw your complete energy into this questioning/exploratory phase. Let your body language and eye contact show that you are really interested in what people have to say. You would hope that the water-cooler chatter would be something like, "What's up with Brenda? She's really wired about this new campaign, what did she ask you?" "I've never seen him so focused on something, what's going on?" or "Man! He is into this!"

As you have these talks with people your picture of their place in the organization will begin to change. It will grow to be more in line with how they perceive themselves. Usually this is as a leader or a specialist of some kind. Typically everyone sees himself or herself as a "team player" even if you don't really see them in that way. Perhaps the most prevalent (and most hurtful) myth of leadership is that leaders are found only at the top of organizations. Businesses need leaders at all levels. In sales offices leadership is needed most in the places where the officers/managers are seen least. These leaders can do things that the Manager or President could never do themselves. Who is the spark plug? Who is the service maniac? Who is the "mouthpiece" for the team? Who is always trying something new? Who is the witty stress-reliever? Who is the office's bullshit detector? Who is Mr. Consistency? Who always has something valuable to add to meetings? We could go on and on. And we should, because the more areas you can find and acknowledge leadership, the more leaders you can have on your team. There is nothing quite as ridiculous as the manager who really believes that they are the most competent at everything there is to do in their organization. What does that say about their training skills, about their ability to develop talent, and scarier still, what does that say about the future of their team?

Now is the time for making positive changes. The best way to begin to influence people's perception of themselves or their value to the organization is to gradually and very persistently affirm their new (and more significant) role. Take time to be with people and explain how you see them expanding their role and their impact in the office as you work towards their (and your) vision. Explain how you feel that they could be a much more influential part of the team and get their feelings about the best way to do this. I have in the past actually apologized to people on my team for not giving them enough responsibility and underutilizing their skills. The key here is to give EVERYONE an important chunk of the vision that they alone are responsible for. It must be tangible (measurable) and more responsibility than they had before. If you can tie an incentive to an expected increase then do it. Any incentive tied to any kind of production increase is a no-risk proposition for you. Incentives should be organized with the full expectation that the goals will be realized and exceeded. NEVER set up an incentive that causes you to even remotely root against one of your people.

Many times the new responsibilities that you can assign to people will be in areas that they themselves have recognized as areas of shortcomings or low performance. Be prepared to discover complete mismatches between people and their area of highest interest. Low performance organizations match people with their "competencies" or stuff on their resume or what they studied in college, high performance organizations can hit warp speed by matching people with their area of passion. Susan types 80 words a minute, can take dictation and is always coming up with crazy and workable marketing ideas. She's an original. Where can she make the most difference on your team? It's your job to find the best way to use her unique combination of talents to help the team. Jimmy is a "geek" who works in the MIS department who also happens to be a fantastic public speaker. Deploying talents (wherever you find them) is a necessary function of leadership.

Through your systematic questioning and talking to your team you will find obvious connections between certain people and the outcomes that they are most interested in. These are areas where their expectations will exceed other peoples and where their leadership is needed. By paying attention to these "matches" you can increase the effectiveness of your delegating and see much more passionate responses from people. If, as you make the rounds, you identify someone that you cannot see playing any important role in the organization you must take action there also. You cannot realistically expect everyone to be a zealot and carry a flag for your team. You can, and should, expect everyone to be interested in team progress enough to want some real responsibility and be excited about the opportunity to be a part of something as ambitious as what you are in the process of building. There must be contribution, belief and enthusiasm. On an enthusiastic team, a single person who refuses to be involved or who makes an effort to ooze cynicism and will keep the team connected to the past. On a high performance team the opposite of positive, creative energy is apathy not negativism. A negative person is usually sellable and will go from skeptic to advocate with equal passion. You can work with them as long as they don't absorb too much attention or energy. This person should be given every opportunity to get excited about what is going on. He should be allowed to watch for a short while to be sure that this (and you) are "for real". If after a reasonable amount of time it becomes clear that they have no real connection to where the team is going then the team should go without him.

It will be obvious to the future-oriented leader that apathy poses a much more significant threat to the team vision. The person who does not even care enough to NOT like what's going on should be vaporized for the good of the team and for the preservation and integrity of the team vision of the future. Thinking leaders will realize that when the cynic is a reasonably high profile person then there is an additional and powerful benefit to a disassociation. It's a way of paying homage to the future, to the grand plan. It has been done this way since medieval times. When you want to call attention to a big initiative you sacrifice something to add drama. Hopefully everyone will get caught up in the idea of creating something special and this won't be necessary. If it is necessary, be decisive and respectful to both the person in question and to the ideas they are threatening.

Two key things to remember:

1. The future is only slightly more exciting than the present. Right now must be seen as a great place to be in your organization. These are the "good old days". People are proud of the things they have already done. Acknowledging prior progress is a great way to build confidence and add horsepower to new movements.

2. Everything affects momentum. You can't allow anything to slow this thing down once it begins taking on a life of it's own. There is nothing that you can't use to strengthen your vision and the pull of the future. With a little forethought a leader can be masterful at making any circumstances, even seemingly catastrophic ones, fit into the long-term vision for the team. If your crew, who are gradually getting sold on the reality of this high-concept, high-performance, high-challenge, high-involvement vision see any lack of spirit or resolve in their leader it will affect them very significantly. It will feed any lingering doubts they have and may make your water-cooler cynic (if you haven't vaporized him yet) look very smart. You must be completely bulletproof. In a crisis you have an excellent opportunity to show poise and resolve. These are the moments of truth. Look forward to them as a way of demonstrating that NOTHING is more important that what we are trying to build here.

Keeping The Atmosphere Pure

It is certainly more challenging to create a great high-energy atmosphere than it is to maintain one. Any organizational culture, be it good or bad, has its own survival instinct and it's own powerful momentum. In thinking of the office atmosphere as the teams "personality" we can see how it would take on it's own momentum and be very easy to maintain so long as people were matched well with objectives and the leader/manager is still paying attention.

One of my favorite metaphors for good leadership comes from the sport of curling. Even if you are completely unfamiliar with the sport (as I am) you have probably seen it on TV. It consists of one guy pushing a really heavy thing hard with a big stick so it slides down this lane while some other guy runs in front of the heavy object with a brush clearing debris and obstacles away so that the other fellows push gets this heavy thing to go as far as possible down the lane. The "pushing guys" are usually really strong and expend a lot of effort just to make the heavy thing go at all. The "brushing guys" generally are quick and lean so that they can keep running ahead of the heavy object and keep the path in front of it clear.

In this metaphor the leader is the guy who is running and sweeping ahead of the sliding object. We are making sure that the great efforts of our pushers are going as far as possible. We want to make sure that our pushers look good and that the results of their efforts make them feel that they have accomplished something, even if we have to run and brush ahead of them like maniacs to insure a favorable outcome. That's leadership! When a leader is doing her job, a good portion of her "management tactics" are just staying out of the way and attending to the details that keep things teams moving forward. A great atmosphere takes care of almost everything else!

What follows are some areas to pay particular attention to once you have established an environment of excellence in your organization:

Atmosphere deflators:

- Low Expectations of any kind (you must find sources of cynicism and attack).

- Softening of Standards (is the organizational objective comfort or performance? You can't work towards both).

- Ghosts of past failures or mediocrity. Get rid of anything in your physical space that can be a reminder of an unproud past.

- Negativism and apathy of any kind. As we have noted, apathy is far more dangerous to your team's general outlook than any negativism could be. Someone who really does not care is very unusual. Clearly, this person has nothing to add to your team if he is genuine in his criticism and not just suffering from a personality disorder. These "bad attitude" people can liven up any conversation and sometimes even represent the majority view. They can say things that others don't want to. Taken in small doses this person can be a very important part of the organization especially when you consider that, in most organizations, this person is a veteran who has seen it all and carries significant credibility with your team. Many times this person will act as a mouthpiece for the dark side. It's far worse if you are leading an organization where nobody ever has anything to say that is out of harmony with the team. That's called a cult and is really scary.

- Over-Intervention by the leader. A leader who must be involved in every decision, every dispute, every happening, is not helping his team. Let the group deal with things as they come. This is how new leaders rise up. This how people learn what their capabilities really are. In some organizations the manager is only person who gets to think creatively. The rest of the team is just supposed to go by policy or by how they have been trained. By not allowing (and applauding) flexible and innovative responses we miss opportunities for growth and the evolution of new answers to old problems. As was stated in the section on "Trust", if you are the only one with any good ideas in your office or division you are soon going to notice that the marketplace is able to accept new solutions faster than you alone can come up with them. No one mind is good enough anymore (even your brilliant one).

Atmosphere Increasers:

- Things that work (effectiveness/success).

- True enthusiasts.

- Strategic (on purpose) diversity. When we talk about diversity these days everyone thinks about gender and race. That should go without saying. I'm talking about diversity in the *kind* of people that are allowed to play a role on your team. Personalities! Managers used to believe that organizational strength came from a scary kind of like-mindedness among the entire team. "We need to be on the same wavelength", they would say. Well, here is one of those areas where nearly the opposite is true. It seems that the more different kinds of people/personalities you have the greater the potential strength and energy you will have. It is the magical friction created by two (or more) completely different viewpoints that spawns the best ideas and solutions. In the old days (ten years ago) groups of suburban 47-year-old white guys would launch products and services and then be amazed at the lack of market enthusiasm or interest. What could they expect? Anything that is conceived is such a narrow frame or perspective cannot really be expected to have a mass-market appeal (except by plain old dumb luck…which does happen). The good news was that the population they were trying to sell to was much narrower that it is today and that gave them a snowballs chance. The next big idea was the focus group. It's easy to imagine how this idea formed. One of the 47-year-old white guys says, "since we seem to be missing large portions of the market why don't we bring in representative groups that we can get opinions from about what they want in our product/service". This idea worked in a limited way but is still far inferior to the concept of your organization actually *being* like the population you were trying to sell to. When services and products are conceived, designed, adjusted, launched and marketed by the very people that are meant to buy it the odds of a big hit go up remarkably. If you want to sell to a lot of different kinds of people you had better BE a lot of different kinds of people.

- A learning Leader. At the risk of repeating myself, there is nothing more important in as a leader than the perception that you are open to ideas, open to conflict and open to criticism. The ideal description would be a leader who is a smart, active listener. Who is open to communication from any direction or any source. A leader who knows that the best ideas haven't even been hatched yet and who seems to be serene and confident about the success of the enterprise. There is this pervasive sense of "authenticity" about the best leaders. They take more pride in being students of the success process than they would ever take in their position or title.

- Positive recognition of ANY kind. The phrase "catch them doing it right" is one of the most important and meaningful clichés in business.

- Heavy involvement of team in everything possible. I have never seen "involvement" overdone. Even when certain kinds of participative decision making feels silly it still counts and has an impact in your organization. How about Sandra the human-resources person helping with the purchase of new office furniture? How about the receptionist reviewing the copy for a new ad you are considering? Should the clerical staff have a voice in choosing a new copier or fax? Would it make sense to have the techies meet the sales guy you are interviewing? It would seem so, but many of these small involvement opportunities are neglected. Members of teams are denied the right to feel connected to the decision making in the organization. I would highly recommend that you be on the "overdoing it" side of involvement rather than on the side of neglect.

Conclusion

In the end, the greatest responsibility of a leader is the responsibility of providing a place where people can come to be excellent. A place where they are caught doing it right. You must create a place where success doesn't surprise anyone. Where great expectations greet them at the door and they have a hand in the deciding the direction the team is headed. The atmosphere of your organization can compel people to re-estimate their potential and future possibilities. It's you job to create it and nothing is more important.

Recognizing Success and Failure Traits in People

One of the things I have enjoyed most about having a leadership position with a successful company is all of the visits I get to make to our different offices. I like to go where the action is, where there is a thriving office with lots of exciting people who seem to be really engaged in what they are doing. It's always interesting to see the contrasts between different offices and divisions, but the most striking aspect about the successful organizations is their relative similarity. In other words, what works in one place works in another. Successful organizations all seem to operate at a similar frequency. I think this is the vibration that occurs when an organization is led by a truly capable leader. It just feels right. The contrary is true too. An office or organization that does not perform well seems to have a certain personality too. I have become so sensitive to these vibrations (for lack of more descriptive word) it has almost come to the point where I believe I could tell you whether a certain office or operation was a successful one just by the feel of it, even without meeting any of the people who make up the organization or seeing any kind of results.

Over my travels and many meetings with business people all over the map, I have come to three key realizations that have formed the cornerstones to my personal business philosophy.

Number one: Intelligent effort is always rewarded. When good people with good intentions do their best at something it is always going to succeed. It may be sooner or it may be later, but success is on its way.

Number two: A leader can actually create an atmosphere that compels performance. Over time, top leaders are able create a place where people will come to be excellent. That place can be an office, a department, a division or a whole company.

Number three: The power of the individual will always prevail. What I mean by this is that success or failure will always come down to a personal decision. Even in the worst of circumstances there are people who will succeed. You will also find people who have been given every possible advantage who still fail to even approach their real potential. The essence of the individual transcends leadership and circumstance. What a leader can do is provide a place where excellence can happen. The leader can create momentum and provide a positive example of success. The leader can set a compelling expectation of results and performance. Even with all of this the ultimate decision about performance and success lies with the individual.

I have organized a list of five critical attributes I have seen demonstrated and repeated among the top business achievers and leaders that I have been able to work with. These are the traits that repeat consistently in people that succeed. These are the traits that leaders should look for when building or adding to their teams. I strongly recommend that you review these and consider them, as I have. Following that list I have included another five-item list of some characteristics I have found that severely limit people. These are some of the attributes that will very likely make a person a liability on your team. You have seen them all before, but they are worth reviewing.

Here are some of the attributes shared among the top performers I have had the opportunity to know and learn from. You know the kinds of people I am talking about—those people who constantly transcend their positions to influence the rest of us. The performers who can always focus, always "will" the proper outcome and who always seem to land on their feet. These people make up a critical minority in any company and we all benefit from their exploits and we tell their stories. It's important to have role models in any business. They help the rest of us to see ourselves crashing through the same walls and leaping the same tall buildings. Businesses need heroes too.

Five attributes of top business performers:

1. They are results oriented. They consider performance a part of their personality. These people are infatuated with what works. Most top achievers spend a *little* time discovering what will allow them to succeed and *lots* of time doing those things, rather than the other way around. They love how reliable the fundamentals are in business. They love being surrounded by other people who know how to make success easy by paying attention to what works. They want to be recognized as reliable performers and respond positively to challenges.

2. They are tough. For some reason, "toughness" does not get mentioned much when success characteristics are discussed. Make no mistake; business achievers are tough as nails. Top performers must work through and around their circumstances. Their lives have the same challenges as anybody else's, they are just driven more by their mission than by their mood. One of the things from which I benefited when I started in business was a total lack of self-deception. My manager went out of his way to explain that success in business (and especially in direct sales where I started) is not easy and certainly not for the weak of resolve. He was right.

3. They have a long time perspective. Top performers do not judge their success or failure with short-term measurements. Short-term metrics are just not reliable for making important decision or key adjustments. They know that they can become very successful by becoming truly excellent at a few disciplines. The great news is that the disciplines you must learn to be successful in a business environment are the very same disciplines (goal setting, ethical behavior, active listening, mental toughness, continuous self-improvement, hard work, results orientation, etc.), which will help them in all the other aspects of their lives as well.

4. They have an entrepreneurial approach to work. They are in business for themselves, but not by themselves. They really are their own brand. They realize that, in order to have a positive impact on their organizations, they must often be able to motivate themselves and operate independent of others. Top performers are essentially running their own personal service corporations. Most very successful people have this kind of entrepreneurial mindset even if they are not actually entrepreneurs. They know what they want to known for and strive live up to their own unique expectations.

5. They have decided to make a difference through their work. They put a heavy value on their "work reputation". They don't just work through the week to get to the weekend. These people clearly feel they have a mission (regardless of their position) and understand where their individual success fits into the overall company's success. Representing a quality company and doing quality work gives them a wonderful opportunity to serve.

Now let's consider the other half—those who can't seem to make things happen. The people who never seem to make any meaningful progress in their careers, and consequently, are real liabilities in their organizations. If we were all paid on the basis of good intentions, these people would be millionaires. They are the "80" part of the 80/20 rule. I have come up with what I think are the five major reasons why people don't reach their potential at their work. You will find people who have these negative attributes at all level of organizations. See if you recognize any of them.

1. People who fall in love with their limits instead of their possibilities. It is easy to be seduced by excuses. Why? Because we all have them. Are mine better than yours? Are hers better than his? It is possible to spend a lot of time thinking about these things. Many people are far more comfortable with the surrender than they are with the work. Deciding to focus on your perceived limits is a choice, just like pursuing goals or improvements is a choice.

2. People are often much more aware of what they don't want to be than what they do want to be. I am constantly hearing people describe (in impressive detail) exactly what they don't want to be. They say they could never be pushy, or self-serving, or money-motivated, dictatorial or a workaholic. I always wonder how incredible these folks could be if they had spent as much time figuring out what they actually would like to become.

3. Forgetting to work on themselves. This is a big one and it is discussed in a few other chapters in this book. To succeed in the fast-paced world we live in now (and enjoy it), we must work on ourselves as hard as we work on our jobs. Incredibly, the act of self-improvement is also your best career move! To be the same as you were five years ago with no new insights, philosophies, or lessons would be the saddest of outcomes. It should be seen as an embarrassment to not be developing. We

all seem to have time for lunch, television, gossip, or cigarettes—why can't we find time to read or think?

4. They look for short cuts. When did the short route become more attractive than the reliable one? I am often stunned by the lengths to which otherwise normal people will go to avoid simple and necessary work. This is another one you will find as often in the executive level as anywhere else. There are people who will invite all kinds of career risk into their lives just to avoid doing some part of what they are paid to do.

5. People who never really decide why they come to work in the first place. We have discuss on these pages that the "why" part of success will always overwhelm the "how" part. It's true. The functions are easy in most job roles. Interestingly, the functions of many careers have barely changed in the last 100 years. The tools have changed drastically and will continue to change. But you can read a book on success written in 1940, and it will still have great (and currently applicable) advice. Why are they here? What meaningful things are they working toward? If they don't know, then the work they are doing will be sub-par and will not improve. Performance needs a context and there is only so much a leader can do.

The two lists above are for generalizing purposes only. I would expect that you would add these learnings to your own personal lists. Successful leaders are constantly considering their experiences with different types of people. This allows them to, over time, accumulate a very valuable sense of who can succeed on their teams. These accumulated people-learnings can be priceless. They allow a leader to put together a high performance team very quickly, or to fix a broken team fast. A Full Contact leader will become known over time primarily as an excellent team builder. Understanding people and what drives them is a necessary study for any serious student of leadership.

The Can't/Won't Crossroads

Managing successfully through disappointing performances can be one of the toughest aspects of leadership. Leaders who routinely carry their expectations high are bound to be disappointed. The ability to manage this kind of disappointment is a necessary skill for any leader intent on building a high-performance organization.

The most difficult disappointments come to us when the business results are at odds with what our personal expectations for people have been. Most leaders are very sensitive to people and develop the ability to "read" them and very accurately project what they may be capable of. The disappointments that come with being wrong about someone's capabilities or intentions can be especially hard to accept because they force us to lower our expectations as leaders—something accomplished leaders are loathe to do.

Leaders get reputations for how they routinely deal with these kinds of disappointments. There are managers who will not alter their high hopes for a person regardless of the amount of performance evidence that contradicts these expectations. We have all worked with managers like this. They end up with a reputation for not being able to see people critically. They are often seen as weak performance evaluators, or worse, as Pollyanna's.

At the other end of this spectrum are those managers who, because of their repeated disappointments with people, overcorrect in the other direction—they become cynical about people and what they are capable of. They consciously lower their estimation of what people can do. Having negative expectations insulates these managers against disappointments. Everyone they see reminds them of someone else who let them down. Poor performances only serve to confirm their low expectations. It's easy to see how this cycle can continue for one of these people-weary and cynical managers.

Full Contact Leaders are not polarized or prejudiced by their experiences with the people they lead. They develop their expectations for people through both qualitative and quantitative judgment. When they are wrong about a person's capabilities or intentions they approach the issue with the goal of improving the situation or learning from it. This is where the Can't/Won't Crossroads can help.

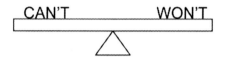

You have a performance issue to resolve. You need to get at the root of the problem so that you can successfully act on it. There is a bottom-line issue underneath all of the extraneous issues that are usually addressed in business settings: Is it the actual capability of the person you were wrong about or was it their intentions? The fundamental question is simply, is it a "can't" or a "won't"? Just knowing the answer to that question can make all of the difference when you are trying to manage through disappointing performances. This can't/won't distinction is what we need to know. These are very different answers that would lead to correspondingly different solutions. What follow is a list of various performance issues where we might apply this question:

- A new salesperson that has not made his target number of prospecting calls in either of his first two weeks with the company.

- A district manager who has not organized effective planning meetings for her team.

- An administrative assistant who is nearly always ten minutes late to staff meetings.

- A service department representative who can't seem to answer the phone before the fourth ring.

- A staff accountant who has turned in sloppy and inaccurate reports several times this year.

- A regional vice president whose annual business plan does not contain any of the initiatives that have been identified as top priority by senior management.

- A consultant who never follows presentation scripting that has proven to be effective.

The examples could go on forever. Wherever there are unexplained performance shortcomings. Whenever there are outcomes that seem contrary to what you, as the leader, expected. Remember, your high expectations of your team members can and will be the strongest positive factor influencing successful behavior. Top leaders should only get surprised "down" at low performance, not "up" at successful outcomes.

So the question to ask is: "Is it that you can't or is it that you won't?" This is a very fair and simple question that gets to the heart of any performance issue.

Let's illustrate how this question can be used with a real-life example. John is new to the team. He has been hired as an account executive. His action plan calls for him to make 200 prospecting calls in each of his first four weeks. This 40-per-day prospecting pace will allow him to schedule a full week of sales presentations. In over 20 years of watching ratios for new people as they begin their sales careers, the company has determined that when new salespeople make their 200 calls each week they will set a solid selling schedule and close enough business to be successful in the difficult early stages of a sales career. The company is so confident in this plan that they even discuss it when they are interviewing and recruiting to make sure that they don't hire someone who does not understand the value of heavy prospecting activity at the beginning of a sales career.

John is in his third week after his initial training. In his first week after training he made 137 calls and set four sales appointments. In week two John made 117 calls and set three appointments. At the end of each week John's manager has reminded him of the 200-call benchmark and how risky it is to try to succeed with a weak selling schedule. To make matters worse, John has confided in his manager that he is nearly broke and needs to start selling fast. The manager is confused. Here is a seemingly intelligent guy who says he needs to do well ignoring the most important success guideline he has been given. The manager has set aside some time to talk with John early in week three.

The manager starts the meeting with a question: "John, I am concerned with your progress so far here with the company. You have fallen short in each of your first two weeks in your prospecting calls. I know you are very aware of our target—200 calls per week for your first month. Yet you have decided to do less than that each week. I think you are an intelligent and capable person…that's why I wanted you on this team in the first place. Here is the question I need you to answer: Are you not making the 200 calls because you can't or because you won't?"

This question will not be answered quickly or without care. The reason for this is because it is a question where both of the possible answers keep the problem (whatever it is) squarely on the shoulders of the person the question is addressed to. There is no opportunity to thrust responsibility back at the manager or the company. If it is a "can't" then the capability of the person needs to be addressed. Is it a training issue? Is he or she the wrong person for the job? Is there some issue in their life keeping them from being able to perform?

If the answer is a "won't" then we are really talking about intentions and, therefore, what is at issue is the basic relationship between the person and the company. A "won't" may mean that there is a real breech in the agreement between what this person was hired to do and what they are actually willing to do.

The can't/won't question will help you navigate through some of your more vexing people issues. The answer to this either-or inquiry will at the least give you a solid stance for understanding, and hopefully solving, key performance shortcomings in your organization.

How to Know if a Person Can Improve

One of the most challenging aspects of managing performance is figuring out when someone is capable of growth and improvement and when they are not. That's where the Can't/Won't question can be so powerful. Another important consideration when analyzing a person's capability for improvement is in their perspective or point of view about their job's responsibilities. How do they feel about the job they are doing? What is their opinion about their own performance? Do they perceive that there are performance barriers or bottlenecks that are affecting their ability to perform at a high level?

Getting an honest and accurate view of someone's real perspective on their job can be a tricky thing, especially when you are their leader or manager. Someone's ability to improve is usually determined by their belief, or lack of belief, that they can get better at what they are doing. If a person really believes they can improve, the job of helping them becomes much easier. In many situations people just say what they think you want to hear. Sometimes a person doesn't believe they can improve at all. The variable that leaders need to pay the most attention to in these situations is the person's perspective about what would really need to change for the results to improve substantially. It usually comes down to whether the person believes that the improvements can be made internally (them) or must be made externally (the situation or circumstances).

If the person believes their results can be improved internally, as a result of developing their skills or taking certain actions, there is a very high probability that their results can and will improve. On the other hand, if our performance-challenged person believes that their outcomes are being limited by something outside of themselves (perceived barriers or negative circumstances) it will be nearly impossible to leverage any performances improvements. Simply put, when people don't think they are the issue there is little chance of improving their performance. For most people this inside or outside perspective is compulsive and habitual. I consider it a "hard drive" part of a person's personality. What I mean by hard drive is that it is not programming (soft ware) but actually how they are built (hardware). Here is a technique that can help you get to the root of the matter.

Internal or External Control

I recommend you meet with the person you are concerned about. One-on-one meetings are at the heart of many of the techniques used by Full Contact Leaders. In your meeting you would tell them you are concerned about their performance and that you feel they could really improve. If the situation is really dire you may need to tell them that their performance must improve to maintain their role in the organization. What ever the truth of the situation is, relate it to them clearly. After some discussion of your expectations you ask the person to make a list. The list should be the top ten things that would improve their performance. Keep your instructions very simple...just write down the top ten things that would increase their performance in their job. Give them a few minutes of privacy to complete their list. When you return, ask them to simply review their list with you. Once the person has shared their list, you tell them you will spend some time considering their list and excuse them until the next time you talk.

Sit down with their list. It is going to tell you whether this person has the capability to improve in their role or not. Go line by line through the list of ten. Next to each point mark either "P" for person or "C" for circumstances. The "P" (I usually just use their first initial) goes against list items that are in the control of the person. These are things that they directly influence like effort, skill, activity, etc. The "C" goes next to any list entry that is not in the direct control of the person. These are circumstances that are outside of their influence. Keeping this exercise as simple as possible, you look over the list and see if this person believes that improvement is mostly up to them, or mostly out of their hands. People who believe that the ability to improve their results is out of their hands cannot realistically be expected to get better. It would be naïve and a waste of effort to organize additional training, mentoring or attention for them. If your person's list shows mostly issues that they can affect and control you have a very good candidate for training or special attention. They can and will improve.

Take a look at the list below. It is a real list made by a sales person on one of my teams. His name was James and his performance was lagging. There were no meaningful signs of improvement or momentum to build on. Here is his list:

1. Selling market is saturated (all of the big companies have already been prospected or sold)

2. Bad office location (my commute is 45 minutes)

3. Prospects don't want to pay on our terms (need to be more creative in our pricing)

4. My selling materials are outdated

5. I am bad at follow-up

6. Pressure from my wife creating stress

7. Sales meetings take up too much of my time

8. I need better prospect lists

9. I don't have good references to use with prospects

10. Negative office environment

When I review the list I ended up putting a "J" (for James) on only two items on his list (numbers 5 and 8) and a "C" on everything else. James clearly thinks that his improvement and eventual success is not in his own control. Put another way, James doesn't show up on his own list! This is a person who is not going to get better because he does not believe he has any ownership in his lack of progress to date. The fault is spread around very well isn't it? His office, his selling market, his wife, his commute, too many meetings, poor materials, the sales terms…all of them conspiring against him. James is an educated and physically attractive person. He is honest and gives a very good sales presentation. In some ways he is full of potential, but the regrettable fact is that he is not going to improve as a sales person in his current situation.

Understanding the Dark Side

Today's experts have many different explanations about why our contemporary culture seems to be so biased to the negative. We blame the media, the stress of two income families, broad and constant access to (bad) news, commuting from the suburbs, etc. The reasons given are varied and often contradictory. One thing is sure: As a leader you must keep yourself out of the "mood business". As discussed in several ways throughout this book, leaders are responsible for their own states of mind. Your mood or personal circumstances cannot fall within the domain of your relationships with your teams. Having bad moods that affect the atmosphere around you is a luxury you give up when you take on the challenge of leadership. Another challenge for leaders is in understanding that a big part of the job of leadership is in creating a work environment that allows (or even compels) people towards a positive state of mind. We know that the best work is always done in a positive, affirming, and optimistic environment (see chapter on Atmosphere). Whether we can agree on what causes the wholesale negativity we see each day is not important. We must agree that is part of our jobs to understand its impact and respond to it sensitively and with forethought. It is for that reason I have tried over the years to learn what I can about what influences the people I interact with and how to help them manage those influences in the most positive way they can.

One of the really dangerous outcomes from this "dark side" to people (their negative reactions to their worlds and circumstances) is how it influences their aspirations. When there are so many more bad examples surfaced and publicized, (especially in the business world), it can become difficult to find really positive or inspiring career aspirations in the individuals your work with. I believe this explains the current state of the so-called Generation X. They are not in some kind careless malaise or an ambition-free fog, they just don't express their ambition in the way that the generations in front of them did. As a group they are very interested in entrepreneurship and career free agency. I believe this is a general reaction to the stereotyped images they have grown up with. The corrupt, cartoonish or just plain boring careerist climbing a corporate ladder is a tired image. I am surprised it lasted as long as it did.

Leaving the sociology aside, one thing is for sure: *most of the people you will be responsible to have spent a lot more time thinking about what they don't want to be than what they do.* They can tell you all of the different types of people they will never be but, in most cases, have very little to say about who and what they really *do* want to be. This is a real challenge to you as a leader. To help them find their career aspirations you will have to be willing to walk with them through the back door, through the negative image they want to avoid to find a positive one they can aspire to. It can be very useful to make a person aware of the fact that their negative images are much more complete than their positive ones are. It can make for a great introductory conversation with someone you believe may have a lot of potential. The most important thing is to understand that not everyone carries around a fully formed career aspiration in his or her heads. This does not mean that they are not talented or driven. It just means that it may take a little more time for them (and you) to fully realize what they can really bring to your organization.

The ability to evaluate growth and improvement opportunities is one of the most valuable skills a leader can develop. Knowing when you have a "can't" and when you have a "won't", knowing when a person has relinquished control over their own results, knowing when intervention will help and when it won't, these are key leadership competencies for the Full Contact Leader. Understanding these strategies will help you make good decisions about your people.

The GUT-Check

Growing productivity consistently over a long period of time is one of the greatest challenges in business. Getting better year after year when you are working with the same people is something very few leaders are able to do. Take a look around your organization. Think about the people you know that have successfully grown year after year in the same situations. By the "same situations" I mean leaders who improve their operations each year while working with the same basic variables (people, products, territories, compensation, etc.). Without an obvious leverage point it is very hard to grow consistently. If you are not expanding, adding products or services, discounting or adding new sales channels, growing a business is a real challenge. This is especially true when the leader is working with the same core group of people year after year.

We have all seen managers become very creative when faced with this situation. They will desperately look for new ideas and initiatives that might help them grow their business. They will try motivational techniques and contests. They will re-focus on a certain business segment and they will obsessively measure and analyze key metrics looking for opportunities for growth that may be hidden.

It is always easier when you are new to a situation to see the opportunity in it. The grass *is* always greener on the other side. This is one of the reasons why it is sometimes necessary to simply find a new leader for an established team when results are flat or shrinking. Pro sports teams do it all of the time. Many of the coaches are switched around in the off-season. They seem to be simply trading places in the interest of change. A coach who was fired for his performance one day, can then be hired by a new team two days later where they will profess the utmost confidence in him. It happens all of the time.

When a skilled leader walks into a new situation they will always see the opportunity first. They don't know about people's limitations yet. They can't see the bottlenecks in the business. They can't see the lid or lids that the previous leader may have perceived. They are not prejudiced against performance in any way. It is for this reason alone that a leadership change is sometimes a great idea. But what if you are the leader who is stuck? What if it is you who has grown the business in the past but can no longer clearly see opportunities for future growth? What then?

The GUT Check

What is a GUT check? A GUT check is what you need when you are in the situation above. You have grown an organization successfully, perhaps over the course of years, and now can no longer see obvious opportunities for growth. You know your people, for better *and* worse, and you have a strong sense of their capabilities. Performance-wise you feel like you know what is going to happen before it happens. It feels like you have bumped up against the ceiling. This is a dangerous place to be because nothing affects business growth as much as the leaders expectations. If they are low, then poor performance is likely to follow.

The GUT check technique is a way to filter through your organization to search for possible growth areas. The process has been shown to illuminate opportunities in organizations that appear stagnant. The G-U-

T stands for Greatest Untapped Talent and, like all reliable techniques, it is an approach to growth that starts and ends with people.

The technique requires the leader to be willing to:

- See the people in his or her organization in a new way.

- Change some of his current communication patterns.

- Commit to real and communicable expectations to people or teams that formerly had not been big contributors.

- Believe that growth can be developed outside of the (historically) most reliable people and areas.

- Take a risk to grow the business.

Greatest Untapped Talent

There are three steps to an effective GUT check in your organization. The steps are designed to work like a gold prospector's pan, to reorient your perspective on your current team to allow the hidden gold (growth opportunities) to surface and show through. To demonstrate the process, I will go step by step through an example. I will describe a practical application using a real-world example.

The example leader is Katie Greenwood. She is a divisional sales manager at Omnicorp. Her territory is the southwestern U.S. and she has 15 district sales offices broken into three regions overseen by three regional sales managers. Each sales office has an average of 5 sales representatives. Katie has been the divisional sales manager for six years. In the first three years she grew sales by an average of 11% per year. For the last three years her sales have been essentially flat. She is planning her targets for next year and is having real trouble getting excited about her division's prospects for growth. Since her bonus compensation is tied to year-over-year growth she is understandably concerned. It's time for a GUT check.

Step One:

Consider your entire team and focus on the level in your organization where person-for-person performance is the most variable. Typically the level with the most opportunity is also the level with the most distance between the top and bottom performers. You want to focus on levels in your organization before you begin to look at individual people. You are looking for growth leverage points.

In Katie's example there are essentially three layers of people in her sales hierarchy. The first layer is made up of her three regional sales managers. They each manage five sales offices. Although they have differing levels of experience, Katie believes that they have very similar skill sets and that all three of them are competent leaders. Their regions perform similarly on a per-office and per-sales-rep basis.

The next layer in Katie's division is her district sales managers. The experience and performance level in this group varies wildly with the top district offices producing over $500,000 in annual sales and the bottom districts producing less than $100,000 in similar sized markets. The differences in the performance of the district offices cannot be traced to the experience level of the managers (there are a few newer district managers putting up really good numbers and a couple of very experienced DM's doing very poorly). It should also be noted that there are examples of both high- and low-performing district managers in each of the three regions.

The last layer of Katie's organization is made up of her sales representatives. This too is a very diverse group made up of experienced sales professionals with large client bases, representatives with less experience who seem to be growing their client lists and improving steadily, representatives who inconsistently sell and are not necessarily improving and new unproven representatives who may or may not develop into performers. Even though everyone in this level has the same performance-based compensation, the differences in the results between the top and bottom performers are massive and cannot be explained by tenure or territory.

Katie's sales division breaks down like this:

Regional Managers > Narrow Performance Variation

District Managers > Wide Performance Variation

Sales Representatives > Very Wide Performance Variation

Katie's perception of her organization is typical in one important way; there is more variation in performance the lower you go in the hierarchy. This creates a real point of leverage because this is also the level where most of the people are.

Katie has identified the layer in her organization with the Greatest Untapped Talent. It is at her sales representative level. She has analyzed effectively and now has a point of leverage to begin working on. She knows that this level in her organization has the most "upside" and knows that the next step is to devise a plan to get more productivity from her under-performing sales representatives. The first step in developing this plan requires more analysis.

Performance Against Capability

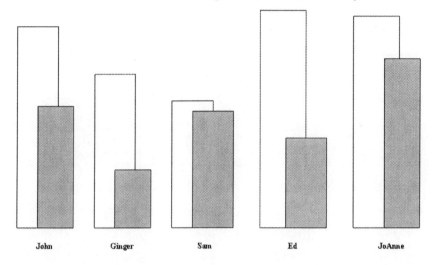

| John | Ginger | Sam | Ed | JoAnne |

Why is the disparity so wide among her sales reps? She knows that all of her regions have many high and low producing representatives so it is probably not a leadership issue. Because the under-performing reps are so widely distributed she knows that the performance issues are systemic, they are part of how her business works.

Step Two

Katie decides she needs to take her analysis deeper by breaking up her sales representatives into levels of seniority so that she can learn more about their performance issues. Here is what she finds:

Reps 0–1 Year	Number—22	Avg Monthly Sales	$5,689
Reps 1–2 Years	**Number—16**	**Avg Monthly Sales**	**$5,520**
Reps 2–4 Years	Number—12	Avg Monthly Sales	$7,846
Reps 4–6 Years	Number—8	Avg Monthly Sales	$9,109
Reps 6+ Years	Number—9	Avg Monthly Sales	$9,458

What Katie is looking for is a group of sales reps that are under-performing and that is a large enough group where a performance increase would make a real difference. Her analysis shows that she does have a group whose sales performance is trailing behind expectations and is not consistent with their level of experience. It is her sales people who have been with her company for between one and two years. She sees that there are sixteen people in this category and that they actually have average sales totals of *less* then the rookie class with less than one year on the job.

Katie's GUT-Check has surfaced an area of opportunity. The opportunity is an obvious training gap in her sophomore class of sales representatives. She sets her performance target at $6,767.50 in monthly sales for her sophomore class. This is half way between the layers of seniority over and under this target class of representatives. This would be a $1,247.50 increase in monthly productivity for 16 people. The annual gain would come to around $239,000, which would make a major difference in Katie's division. She decides to call this group of reps her "growth team" and sets up a meeting with her regional and district managers to discuss what they can all do to increase the sales productivity from this key group.

Katie's GUT-Check has surfaced a clear area of focus. Now she knows what she has to do. With a combination of additional training, new specific sales targets and top-down accountability she will see a meaningful gain from finding and leveraging her division's greatest untapped talent.

This practical example stands to demonstrate that evaluation techniques and analysis tools are important to leaders who must find growth opportunities. Full Contact Leaders learn how to identify leverage opportunities and then develop plans to take advantage of them. The GUT-Check is just one effective technique for doing just that.

Managing Leadership Stress

Managing stress as a leader is critical. As we have discussed, in leadership you do not have the luxury of being grumpy for a day or being volatile in front of your people. Those are indulgences that you can no longer claim when you are charged with leading people. Many people will never become truly effective leaders or have responsibility for others simply because they cannot hold themselves together well enough.

It is not possible to eliminate stress from your world so the only constructive way to approach the topic is to examine where personal stress comes from and then reflect on ways of managing it. For most leaders stress comes from three distinct sources. Studying these sources is the first step in learning how to deal positively with the stress you may feel in your job and life. For many leaders, simply figuring out where their stress is coming from helps them to manage it.

Having an external locus of control

Having an external locus of control is the psychologist's way of describing a person who looks outward for approval. This person may be a very capable person in every other way and, over time, develop a need for outside approval in order to feel good about themselves or the job they are doing. Many leaders develop an external locus of control because they need to satisfy so many people. When you consider the leader's need to be sensitive to their teams, to perform for their bosses, to be attentive to their spouses and to have quality time with their kids, it is easy to see where the stress would come from. It is hard to keep all of these different people satisfied. Because of this, many leaders begin to feel good about them selves to the extent that they can please others, thus, an external locus of control.

A good way tell how a person is psychologically constructed is to ask the simple question "how do you know when you have done a good job?" The first response will tell you whether they have an internal or external locus of control. If they say, "I know because I feel good about myself" or "I feel proud to have accomplished something" they are self-satisfiers are able to feel successful without other people telling them they are successful. On the contrary, if the question "how do you know when you have done a good job?" is answered with something like "my boss tells me so" or "I get an award" or "I earn my bonus" then you know the person is someone who wants to the outside world to tell him that he or she is successful.

Over time adults develop a veneer over their real personalities. It is a veneer that allows them to get along with and satisfy the people in their lives. This veneer is both necessary and inevitable. The people that don't ever develop it end up on the streets or worse. It is an important part of the polite society of which we are a part but it is not actually "you". The part that is you is on the inside. It is the you that is your internal dialogue. The "you" that is your values and your capacity to love. This is your truest self.

There is a term from the art world called "pentimento". Pentimento is a process that occurs over time in oil paintings. It was not uncommon for painters in the past to paint over a painting that they did not like or were not satisfied with. Even some of the old masters repainted their canvasses. Over a period of many years it was discovered that the original painting would start to show through the re-painted image on the same canvass. When many more years passed the original painting would even overtake second painting as the primary image you could see in the frame. This process is called pentimento, because the painter "repented" and changed his mind. It has even happened with some highly regarded classical masterpieces. I liken that original painted-over image as your true and best self. Over time a leader's real persona will come to the surface just like in the ancient paintings. That real image is the one that can be satisfied with it's self. That person does not rely on popularity of satisfying others to feel good. He feels good because he is good (and that is good enough).

Examining where your satisfaction comes from is important, especially if you are feeling high levels of stress. It may be that you have allowed too much of your self-image to fall into the hands of other people.

Doing less than you can

Another big source of stress among high achievers and leaders is the idea that they are doing less than they can. Most leaders consider themselves to be highly capable performers who can produce at a high level all of time. Realistically this is almost impossible to do. Many leaders put intense pressure on them selves to perform at an incredibly high level all of time without making any compromises. It is this prototypical highly ambitious and competitive A-type leader who is most likely to experience the kind of stress that comes from being unrealistic about their capability.

A person cannot be "on" all of the time. It is not even in a leaders best interest to try. Leadership is about balance. The leader must be able to know when it is time to turn things up and when its time to use the brakes. Deliberately slowing yourself down can be one of the hardest things for a highly driven professional to do. The leader must understand that every meeting is not "the" meeting, every month is not "the" month and every presentation is not "the" presentation. Effective leaders have perspective and learn that the ability to demonstrate this perspective is as important for their followers as it is for them selves.

Managing an organization you will have 1,000 little "moments of truth" each week. Some are big and some are little. It is important to be able to differentiate them. Here are a few areas of confusion that can knock an otherwise capable leader out of balance:

The difference between:

- Busyness and productivity.
- Hard work and performance.

- Completion and accomplishment.
- Being motivated and being hyperactive.

Your people depend on you to model both goal-orientation and balance. Sometimes that means pulling back on the accelerator a bit. Allow yourself to do this and your team's overall performance will increase while your personal stress level decreases.

Thinking about Yourself

"The greatest cause of stress is thinking about yourself". I remember where I was the first time I heard that sentence. It was at a leadership seminar being held outside of Atlanta in the mid 1990's. The topic under discussion was stress and where it comes from. I did not accept this statement at first. I simply wrote it in my journal to consider later. I have thought about it many times since then and I eventually realized that it is absolutely true. It is true in my life and it is true for all of the people I know that will tell you that they are highly stressed. It has become almost fashionable to be "stressed out" and to say so when someone asks you how you are doing. It is definitely a narcissistic comment because it then falls to the asker to query; "really? why?" and then the stressed person gets to list their unique challenges and issues.

I wonder why being calm, peaceful and serene is not fashionable. It seems like it would be. But instead everyone wants to claim that they are busy and stressed. As a leader you have to think clearly about what is actually going on. It's true, stress *is* caused by thinking about one's self. Things are not going the way you hoped they would go, you have not had enough time to something you want to do, you are not getting any positive attention from your boss, you are worried about missing your bonus, you are suspicious of the new guy they just brought in, you are stressed because the month is looking bad, etc. A leader cannot not get tangled up in this kind of thought and still be able to be responsive to his team and his family. Simple worry is probably the biggest root of stress. Justifiable worry that your condition will worsen in some way and the kind of fictional worry that centers on things that will never happen. Earl Nightingale said, "worry is the misuse of the imagination". I believe that most types of stress could fall under that same definition.

The best way to escape from self-centered stress is to get busy doing things for other people. Actively seek out people in your organization to help and teach. Pull your attention off of your own condition. The truth is that feeling and expressing stress are not going to help anything anyway. We all have legitimate worries that should be taken seriously. Take those seriously. The rest of what we call stress is just noise. It is the noise the real world makes and it is not going to go away. The best course of action to try to make a positive impact on as many people as you can. Do this and the noise will be much harder to hear.

Toxic Beliefs

As I have studied businesses and people over the years it has become clear to me that organizations excel to roughly the degree that they believe in the possibilities and potential of their people. That sounds like a hopeful platitude that you might find on a motivational poster somewhere, doesn't it? Give it some thought, and apply the concept to some of the businesses that you are familiar with. Organizations that allow and promote a diversity of opinion, accept mannerly disputes, acknowledge excellence wherever it is found (from the mailroom to the boardroom) and share information liberally generally have a higher level of person-for-person productivity than those bureaucratic organizations where upper management consistently underestimates their own people's capabilities. There are quantitative metrics available that actually show comparative per-person revenue in organizations. You can imagine the disparity between the firms where people are allowed (and expected) to grow in responsibility and challenged to improve and those organizations where people are kept in categories and classifications that management has predetermined.

Slow growth (and no-growth) businesses and their leaders are often hampered by what I call "toxic beliefs". These are beliefs that exist in a business that are actually poisonous to the growth and success of those businesses. Sometimes these beliefs are ancient biases and prejudices that have been handed down from old leaders. In other cases they are beliefs that have taken on a life of their own simply because no one has made the effort to properly surface and disprove them. Here are some toxic beliefs that exist in business organizations today. You may recognize some of them as being familiar.

- People will do as little work as they can possibly get away with
- People are looking for ways to take advantage of management
- We must emphasize rules more that we emphasize opportunities
- People are what they are. They don't change
- Full disclosure is not an option
- Our organizational chart mirrors our people's intellectual level
- People only work for money
- The numbers will tell us all we need to know
- Protecting ourselves from our people is a top priority
- We talk like a democracy but act like a dictatorship

It is easy to see why any one of these viral beliefs could handicap a leader or a business. One of the traits of successful leaders is the ability to self-examine. To look into their own heads for beliefs they may have that could have become outdated, obsolete or perhaps were never true but were believed anyway. I call this process the "leadership CAT scan".

The Leadership CAT Scan

Just like a medical CAT scan, the leadership CAT scan is a way to objectively examine your own current beliefs about your team or situation.

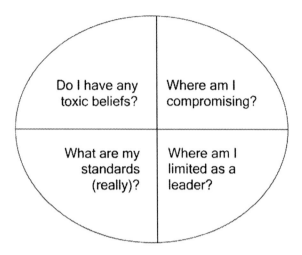

Asking yourself tough questions like these will help you to discover any errant predispositions or prejudices before they begin to affect how you lead your people.

Doing the Right Thing in the Wrong Way

Many of the beliefs that can hurt us the most as leaders have to do with some of the most routine aspects of running a business or even a department. How we introduce a new person into the organization, how we promote someone in a way that is positive for the rest, how we handle losing someone, how we let someone go, how we deliver bad news, how we communicate change, etc. These are the things that ordinary managers do not give a lot of thought to. They will inadvertently cause fear or angst in their organizations and not be sensitive enough to see the origin of the negative feelings. One of the best habits to get into is talking to someone on your team before communicating something important or sensitive. Tell someone how you intend to deliver the message and see what he or she thinks. Their impression of how a communication will be received is almost always more accurate that yours will be, plus it's a great way to show a person that their opinion is valued.

Recently, in a company I am familiar with there was an abrupt dismissal of a key executive. The person let go was the CFO and had always seemed like a trusted and tenured part of the executive team. He was a high-profile person and known well by many people in a large corporation. The announcement was made from the company president in a conference call with his executive team in this way: "effective immediately, Joe CFO is no longer with (the corporation). We are interviewing replacements and you will all be apprised when we make a hiring decision. Does anyone have any questions?" Sometimes executive decision-making is so questionable that there can be no questions.

A message delivered in this way has wide-reaching consequences. The president, not realizing the cost of a hasty (and clumsy) communication, was not aware of the following repercussions:

- It was he who had built up the former CFO's influence and credibility with the rest of the management team. When he does this again with the new (replacement) CFO, he will sense the skepticism that he caused with his abrupt termination.

- Other seemingly important executives become very aware of their dispensability as a result of the President's cavalier handling of a major change in the executive team. Fear is possibly the most debilitating emotion for people. Why create it when there may be no reason to do so? When reasons for a dismissal are given people rest assured that their circumstances may be very different that the departed CFO's. If the reasoning is confidential then that is all that needs to be said, everybody will "get" it.

- Using the words "effective immediately" is harsh-sounding and calls into question the departing CFO's credibility. If a firing is "with cause" it should be noted. If not, then insinuations should not be made with careless language. This is especially true when "the departed" has been a valuable part of the team. It is possible to upgrade a position without downgrading the previous person.

In scenarios like the one above the word "careless" it the most appropriate description of how the decisions are made. Without care. Without care for the departing persons reputation. Without care for the feelings and insecurities of the rest of the team. Without care for his (the Presidents) own reputation and trustworthiness. Changes happen. People lose their jobs. Everyone knows this. Forethought and good judgment become all the more important when managers are expected to deal with the negative inevitabilities of business.

The Truth about Truth

One of the most toxic beliefs found in leaders and organizations today is that you can't be forthright and truthful with the people who work for your company. They believe that broad disclosure of operating strategies (and the associated numbers) shouldn't be known by the rank and file. These same executives will sit around and wonder where employee loyalty has gone or why their Gen-X hires don't seem to rally around the company slogan. One of the most interesting attributes about the current business environment in America is how easy it is to impress people with honesty. Employees, peers, customers, everybody is impressed when someone is very honest. Honesty is even referred to as a "strategy" in some contemporary business writing. The upshot is this: people who are honest by nature are (finally!) at a real advantage. Telling the truth when its not easy or telling the truth when it sets you back in the short-term demonstrates a strength of character that is now considered rare.

The phrase "telling the truth" is very compelling. These days, the part that of that phrase that counts is the telling. "Knowing" the truth is easy, everybody does. This ability to *tell* the truth has been made to seem perilous in many modern business environments. Especially when that truth may get in the way of today's profits or if that truth contradicts what numbers people are trying to get the numbers to say. There are companies whose policies directly oppose their mission statements. There are firms who preach customer centricity when their actual business strategies demonstrate that customer service is a non-priority. There are companies who preach an employee-first philosophy while planning their next downsizing.

People who have the ability and integrity to speak up about the reality of a situation or condition are the key to improving a business. I would never recommend unnecessary criticism or provocation as a career strategy, but I would suggest that becoming known as a person who can consistently discern and communicate the truth in key situations is a very valuable person in today's business world.

The belief that business leaders cannot fully disclose and be overtly sincere with their teams is one of the most toxic beliefs. All that followers expect from their leaders is reliability and sincerity. The word sincere comes from the Latin phrase sine cera, which literally means "without wax". They used the term to describe fine statues. In the ancient world when a sculptor made a mistake on a marble statue they would fill in the area with wax to try to pass it off as a top quality work. Those fine statues that were sculpted entirely without wax were described as being "sine' cera". That's what our followers want from us, sincere leadership without wax.

Soft Skills and Bifocals

Why have traditional people skills fallen by the wayside in the modern organization? Why does that represent a special opportunity for us? We will address these questions in the next few pages.

It used to be that a person would rise in a corporation as far as his or her work ethic and people skills would take him. It's just not true anymore. That's not just old-school nostalgia. It is a fact. The work ethic piece is still necessary, perhaps more than ever, but the people skills part is not. Experts say that there are more key executives who have risen from technical or finance/accounting roles than ever before. Paying attention to trends in executive succession lines has always been a great way to judge what is being valued in the business world. There was a time when most key executive rose up from the sales ranks. Today your president or CEO is more likely to be an accountant or IT person. That does not necessarily mean that they don't have people skills, in fact, most do. It means their management biases will usually go in the direction of the executive expertise. In the accountants/executives case, she will most likely manage through and with the numbers. The IT expert will also be more likely to make decisions in the direction the data points him. Take a look at your own organization. Who is running it? What do they value? How do they measure value? Is that measurement consistent with your own?

Before we talk about how these trends are influencing everyday business, there are a couple of myths we should discuss. These are a couple of myths that each successive generation of business people want to assign to their particular era. It is important to understand these myths and expose them for what they really are.

Myth #1: There is more competitive pressure than ever.
False. There has always been intense competitive pressure. Yes, we have international competitive pressure but with it comes a correspondingly larger market to sell to. Interlopers have always been there. Whether it was carpetbaggers from the north, mail order sellers form Europe or the new blacksmith in town who is setting up on the opposite corner. Competition has always existed. Price competition has always existed and labor competition has always existed. Competition is the biggest part of business and always has been.

Myth #2: The impact of technology is greater than ever.
False. Computer and information technology are only the biggest technologies today. Imagine dealing with the impact of the steam engine, the assembly line, mechanized factories, railroad shipping, etc. There will always be a "next" technology. Fifty years from now our "cotton gin" technology will look quaint to that generation of businesspeople. They will imagine that their market is the most competitive ever (think of intergalactic competition and the robot labor force delivering virtual services…YIKES!).

It isn't technology and competition that is influencing our current lapse in personal leadership. It is the priorities and measurements being set by de facto leaders who are more comfortable managing at a distance, through the data. This is the antithesis of Full Contact Leadership and it can be perilous for any organization that can't see that it is happening or break away form it. The root problem is managing by quantification. Using numbers to make decisions. Attempting to use data to get to know people. Trying to inspire people with numbers. Using them to confuse targets with purpose. Numerically quantifying talent and potential. There are things that numbers can do and things that numbers can't do. Knowing which is which will be one of the key attributes of the successful leaders of the future. Easy access to data and key measures are a huge advantage for the modern managers. It is the over-reliance on these measures that limits many leaders.

Have you ever heard the boiling frog metaphor? It is an oft repeated (but hopefully yet unproven) story of how a frog placed in a pan of water over a flame will never jump out because the change in temperature is so gradual he never reacts. He just sits there in the pan. The same frog, if dropped in water that was already very hot, would immediately jump out of the pan. The sad implication in scenario #1 is that our frog would just sit there and die because he could not sense the gradual change and take appropriate action.

Why would I tell you this story (and fill your head up with this boiling frog imagery)? I think many of our quantitatively based, numbers-first executives may be boiling frogs. Potential, talent, inspiration and motivation can't be found on a spreadsheet. There is no formula that can quantify what talent X inspiration actually equals. A full contact leader know that talent X inspiration = Greatness. The Full Contact Leader knows this formula is just as reliable as your companies' earnings formula or its production-per-headcount measures.

Imagine our frog is using his quantitative skills to figure out when to jump out of the gradually heating pan. He figures that the pan is heating at a rate of 5 degrees every 10 seconds. He figures 5 degrees is no big deal, I can handle that. He is thinking short-term, the real question is what that pan is going to feel like in 30 minutes, but the frog's thinking is set on interim expectations, not the long term effect and soon he is in big trouble. Over-relying on his short-term measurements he does not account for the acceleration of the change in temperature and soon he is cooked. While acknowledging the power of data and the indisputable usefulness of easy-access metrics, we can also point to the proven dangers of being an overly quantitative leader.

#1—Short-term thinking.

As illustrated by our unfortunate frog, using short-term measures to make critical long-term decisions can be unreliable. I have seen many executives use short-term measurements to decide whether some initiative was "working" or "not working" and seen bad decisions made on both sides of the ledger; thinking something was working that was not and, in other cases, thinking something wasn't working when it was. Sometimes the data just doesn't tell the whole story. In most cases the number can't get to the "soft" influences in business. Sometimes these soft influencers are most responsible for what is really going on. Some of these influencers are:

Morale	Commitment	Support
Inspiration	Buy-in	Confusion
Timing	Momentum	Lethargy
Boldness	Saturation	Will

Nearly all of the above are immeasurable and can have a massive impact, sometimes even a decisive impact on whatever you are trying to accomplish in a business. Being a Full Contact Leader means being unafraid to consider and weigh the ethereal and the non-quantitative.

#2—Leadership myopia and the failure to use the big words and think the big thoughts.

The main danger of being a quant-jock (a term I have heard used to describe numbers-manipulation wizards) is succumbing to myopia. Business myopia is a problem with a leaders vision. They see things that are up close (short-term) with perfect clarity. The myopic leader has a lot of trouble with their distance (long-term) vision. This is a real liability because it affects his or her ability to do the one thing that only a leader can do for a business—inspire. When you think about and see only things that are up close you lose the ability to scan the horizon. You become uncomfortable talking about things like purpose, vision and destiny. Those concepts just don't show up in the next quarter, which is as far as the myopic leader can see.

Myopia also affects your rear view; keeping leaders from remembering the lessons found in their businesses histories. This short view can become a critical handicap for a leader and can actually endanger a business. What makes leadership myopia even more dangerous to businesses is that the affected leader is often the only one that is unaware of the problem.

I was fortunate to be a part of a small team that was to decide the long-term focus of a business that had been taken over by new ownership. The business was healthy but adrift. There had been five changes in leadership in the previous eight years. At a branch level (where the real business was being done) there were driven people doing good work. What had suffered was the company's collective identity. There was a lot of "good old days" nostalgia and no real sense of purpose or excitement about the future. The business was running on momentum alone and the numbers reflected that fact.

The meeting included a few very-tenured company field executives along with the new leaders installed by the new ownership. It was a very good team of smart people with the best of intentions. The long-term employees were very passionate about what this company could become. This was the very reason why they had stuck it out through all of the volatility. They really believed the company could be great and important. The new imported leaders got caught up in the passion and together they agreed on a bold new purpose for the business: This company would leverage its entrepreneurial culture and street-level horse-power to become the acknowledged leader in its industry. It already had the product, the footprint and talent (which are usually the hard parts) and only need a good long-term plan and inspired leadership to begin the climb towards its destined position—a dominant brand. So far so good, right? Everybody flew home filled with excitement and anticipation. "We are finally going to kick this organization into high gear," the veterans said to their teams. "The good old days" are still ahead of us.

A few weeks passed. The new executives appropriately busied themselves meeting people and getting to know he organization. They necessarily met with accountants and controllers, learning their way around the numbers. The time came to begin to communicate the vision to the broad team. A whole company call was set up with a web presentation set to go real-time with everyone. The call got off to a great start with business plans and goals shared with the whole team. The call was to finish with the sharing of the company's visions for the future. Here is what it had become: "The company is an industry leader with revenues over $500 million, annual growth of 10%, and earnings greater than 15%." Myopia had set in and ruined a fantastic opportunity to lead and inspire.

When questioned by the company veterans about what had happened to the inspiring statement of purpose they had all crafted together the executives said all of the predictable things. "It needs to be measurable." "We must be accountable to earnings at a branch level." They had lost sight of the horizon. They had, in those few weeks, convinced themselves that everyone would be inspired by the numbers that had inspired them.

By emphasizing the numerical targets the new "vision" satisfied the suits and lost the real producers. What does the sales applicant say to her husband after the interview? "It looks like a good opportunity. I can make a lot of money and this company intends to have earnings in excess of 15%." Leadership myopia begins by affecting the vision of the leader. It quickly spreads to affect the leaders vocabulary. The big words are the first to go. Passion, destiny, purpose, love, greatness, mission, dominance. The words that move people are obscured and fall into disuse. After a time, a myopic leader will actually become embarrassed and self-conscious when these words are used.

A good metaphor for leadership vision is a rudder on a ship. The longer and deeper the rudder the straighter the boat will travel towards its destination. A short rudder will make any watercraft susceptible to small waves and crosscurrents. It will be very hard to steer and keep on course. Taking much longer to reach its destination if it gets there at all. The vision analogy is obvious and accurate.

A Full Contact Leader needs bifocals; he needs to be able to focus clearly on both short and long-term targets. He needs to be able to set up quantitative goals to measure progress against interim benchmarks. Being a bifocal leader means understanding how an inspiring picture of the future keeps people working hard and working happy in the present. A clear vision of the future is one that anyone in your organization can understand how he or she fits in to. The back-office staff, the executives, the accountants, the sellers, the servicers. Everyone. An inspired vision of "what we can become" can actually pull people in, multiply their effectiveness and compel them forward. This kind of shared vision actually takes on a motive force of it's own. It is a leaders responsibility to boldly articulate where everyone is going and how we are going to get there.

When a leader knows how to embrace and articulate both the long and short-term focus of the business they create energy and belief that can carry an organization to heights that simply could not be reached in any other way.

A Declaration of Interdependence

This is a shift in perspective that is necessary for any of us to approach our full potential as leaders. It is a difficult shift in perspective, a shift in the direction of humility. Leadership humility has been discussed in a few other places in this book. It has a critical role in the process of becoming a Full Contact Leader.

To be a truly effective leader you must truly value the people on your team. When I say, "truly value," I mean really understanding that they can do things you can't or won't do. On the human scale we are all equals. On the organizational scale the leader necessarily has a broader span of responsibility, but the org chart is not the scale we are addressing. This kind of humility is not often found in leaders. Most of us actually found our way into leadership positions because of our ego-drive. To earn the kind of trust and belief you will require to drive peak performance with your team, you will need to develop this kind of leadership humility. It is one of the non-negotiable philosophical underpinnings of Full Contact Leadership.

So how do you get there? How do you develop the kind of humility that demonstrates to your staff that you really understand your role and respect theirs? It starts with an acknowledgement of who works for whom. This kind of acknowledgement in an organization does a lot of good. It sets a very democratic tone without an attempt to sell your team on a participative management model that everyone knows is not going to happen. Being democratic does not mean the leader is not accountable to direction and results. Truthfully acknowledging who works for whom also breaks down the fictional and debilitating "everybody works for the boss" idea.

My first leadership role was as a district sales manager in Raleigh, North Carolina. I had a small team comprised mostly of young college graduates. We are all about the same age. The only thing that distinguished me from my team was my title. At first I tried to use that title to manufacture productivity. Like most young leaders, I enjoyed my title and imagined that it was a very important difference between me and "my" team. It did not take long for me to realize that managing by title creates a "please the boss" environment that is not productive at all. It caused all sorts of problems; different levels of productivity when I was there than when I wasn't, gossip and people "telling" on each other and the errant belief that their job security was mostly rooted in their relationship with me. All of these were serious impediments to productivity.

I decided to have my first "who works for whom" meeting. We all sat down and after a short discussion came to understand our real roles and responsibilities. They realized that, as commissioned salespeople, they worked for their prospects and clients. Not for their sales manager. The prospects and clients paid their bills and would make the final decision about whether they succeeded as sales people or not. We also realized that I, as the leader, actually worked for them. I was literally paid by them (overrides on their commissions) and would succeed or fail as a leader based on their productivity. There was no way around it; I worked for them. This understanding was a big step for me as a leader. I could either embrace the truth and use it to move my organization forward, or I could stay true to my ego and force my team to play along with my fictional sense of superiority.

This leadership superiority conceit has been responsible for much of the distance that exists between leaders and their people. This "authority gap" is unnecessary and a presents a real risk to your organization. It can block the flow of trust and ideas between you and the people on your team who will be responsible for getting the important work done.

How do you eliminate this gap and move your team in the direction of trust and interdependence? Here is a short list of simple changes and ideas I recommend for closing the gap:

- Share problems and issues with your team. Don't be afraid of bad morale. Nothing is worse for morale than the collective sense that you are not sharing important information. Assume that they value their jobs and roles just as much as you do. Transparency is your ally in building trust.

- Keep your door open. Unless the conversation is absolutely private there is no reason for closed-door conversations in business. We are all here to succeed.

- Humility can mean a lot of things. Small acts mean a lot. Make the coffee, leave the best parking spot for someone else, make sure someone's chair is comfortable, work in the common work areas. Don't always think your story is most important, don't "one-up" people under any circumstances. You are the boss. You get paid more. That is enough.

- Surprise people with involvement. Ask opinions about issues outside of their responsibility. It shows people that you don't always think you have the best answers. Guess what? You don't.

- Think about the ways you hold yourself above your team. Then think about the reasons why. Challenge yourself and make some changes where you can. They all count.

Acknowledging the interdependence of your team is one of the most powerful steps you can take as a leader. It requires a detachment from ego and the embracing of humility. It means relating to your staff as peers who just have different responsibilities to the organization. This kind of democratic "team", free from the constraints of ego and position, will always out-perform a traditional boss-subordinate arrangement. This acknowledgement of interdependence is at the heart of Full Contact Leadership.

Conclusion

I want to first thank you for spending some time with this book. I tried my best on these pages to share the most important ideas and techniques I have learned and used in my career as a leader and I fervently hope that you feel your attention to these pages has been justified.

I have always considered myself a student of leadership. I know that the coming years will be full of lessons and experiences that I can continue to draw from. I fully intend to keep gathering notes and thoughts on leadership. Check back in a few years, perhaps there will be more to discuss.

I would welcome any thoughts or impressions you may have of this book. I would be especially interested in hearing about your experiences using any of the techniques found in these pages. My email address is schmader@ix.netcom.com and I would truly love to hear from you.

In conclusion, I would like to state that I believe that the Full Contact Leader is the leader of the future. Tomorrow's leader is the one who can answer to the challenge of remaining authentic to them selves while successfully leading others. Decide today to show up as someone new. Someone prepared to lead and not just manage. Someone eager to learn new things and willing to engage people on a person-to-person basis.

I challenge you to begin acting today like the leader you intend to become. It is never too late to become a Full Contact Leader. It can all start today. I wish you the very best in your quest to becoming the best leader you can possibly be.

978-0-595-40592-3
0-595-40592-4

Printed in the United States
66244LVS00004B/409

9 780595 405923